CU00407204

THE MEDICAL GARDEN

Learn about the benefits of herbal medicine and
how to use it effectively also Get insights into the
history and development of herbal remedies

Ted WhitWorth

GET YOUR FREE E-BOOK!

Do you want to escape the unending cycle of pharmaceutical drugs and feel truly healthy? Then give nature a chance. Find out how beautiful-looking herbs can cure and prevent diseases and how to use herbs effectively by signing up for your free copy today!

VISIT: www.tedmedicinal.com

Table of Contents

INTRODUCTION 3

CHAPTER ONE: HOW TO START AND CARE FOR A MEDICINAL GARDEN 6

How Do You Begin A Herbal Medicine Garden? 6

Herb Selection and Growing 9

CHAPTER TWO: BENEFITS OF HAVING A PERSONAL APOTHECARY GARDEN IN YOUR HOME 16

What Is A Home Apothecary? 16

Benefits Of Having A Personal Apothecary Garden In Your Home 32

CHAPTER THREE: HEALING HERBS WITH THEIR USES AND HOW TO HARVEST THEM 35

CHAPTER FOUR: PRESERVING YOUR HERBS 236

How To Preserve Fresh Herbs 236

Conclusion 243

INTRODUCTION

Nowdays, finding medicinal herbs is easy. There are prominent displays of capsules and tablets, tinctures and oils, branded with names of both common and uncommon plants, in health food stores, organic food co-ops, and even regular grocery and drugstores. Alongside the usual black teas and coee are herbal teas. The claims have been dramatic in the case of a select herbs, such as ginkgo as a memory aid, with promises exceeding either traditional applications or scientific evidence. Herbal medicine has evolved into a lucrative industry, and as a result, we run the risk of losing sight of its original purpose. Indigenous healers had to recognize, gather, and prepare the herbs they believed to be useful. They were aware of the plants' growth cycles, as well as when and how to harvest various plant components. Today's commercial herb industry participants are equally knowledgeable. Occasionally, their products serve as a reminder of their natural, earthy roots: The cayenne pepper powder stings the tongue, the aloe gel oozes thickly from the bottle, and the goldenseal powder shines a mustard yellow.

Today's herbal remedies, however, are frequently made to avoid overstimulating the senses: "Experience the miraculous powers of garlic without any aftertaste!" Understanding how to use medicinal plants and other healing herbs can only make their use as a part of our culture in the future more valuable, efficient, and long-lasting. Plants have a long history with health and medicine. Plants' unique function in health and wellness includes both the foods we consume and most of the medications we use. Today, over 40% of medications used to treat human diseases in the United States are derived from plants or were originally derived from plants. Why would you be interested in learning how to plan and grow a medicinal herb garden? With more and more people choosing out of the usual this or that, there has been a surge in interest in gardening in general, and growing herbs in particular, in recent years.

Even if you aren't ready to employ herbs to improve your health and wellness, they are incredibly helpful plants in the landscape. Most herbs are not difficult to cultivate, have beautiful flowers and/or intriguing leaves, and may be readily included into your perennial beds or any classically manicured space. Many herbs grow well in pots, whether inside or outdoors, and most of them are q uite adaptable to different climates and soil types. Many herbs are actually pest-resistant plants! Even those who don't like herbs are familiar with the fundamentals, such as basil, mint, and garlic.

Surprisingly, all these three are classed as culinary and medical herbs, meaning they are both extremely nutritious and tasty, as well as powerfully effective in treating a variety of health conditions. A medicinal herb garden is one grown with the intention of meeting the needs of your overall health maintenance and any acute issues that may emerge. Herbs have numerous uses. Plants known as medicinal herbs can assist your general health. Positive outcomes of scientific research confirm the timeless knowledge of our predecessors. Herbs are easily transformed into tinctures, topical treatments, and beverages. The distinction between a culinary and therapeutic herb might be hazy at times. Take mint as an example. It is freq uently used to flavour summer drinks, salads, and even chewing gum.

Additionally, mint is well known for treating indigestion and stomach pain. Often, the simplest plants to grow are herbs. They are adaptable and do well in most soil types. Herbal remedies benefit from a garden bed that has been amended with old compost. Dig a small amount of sand into your thick clay soil to improve drainage. Most plants don't enjoy having damp feet. The garden may have a specific location for herbs. For perennial and annual herbs, culinary herbs, many of which are annuals, and medicinal herbs, you can pick various sites. Furthermore, it makes good atheistic reason to plant herbs in a floral garden. Many have lovely flowers that are good for pollinating insects, like echinacea.

One discovers new levels on which herbal medicine can enrich our lives and culture as well as heal our bodies by realising that a specific substance, whether delivered in a pill or a capsule, a tube or a bottle, derives from a plant with distinct growing habits and a native range somewhere specific on the globe. We may use these incredible herbs more accurately and responsibly and maintain our health while gaining more information. Throughout the chapters, you will discover everything you need to know about starting, caring for, and especially planting your health herb garden.

CHAPTER ONE: HOW TO START AND CARE FOR A MEDICINAL GARDEN

I'm here to assist you as you begin a garden of medicinal herbs. Usually, the reason people start homesteading is to increase their independence level. Getting a few chickens and perhaps some goats is the typical appearance. But the one thing that surprises me the most is how quickly many homesteaders dismiss the idea of establishing one of the most significant additions to their property—a medicinal herb garden. Taking control of your healthcare is just as crucial as controlling your food system if you're homesteading in order to gain more control over your diet and become less dependent on a system. The best thing you can do is grow herbs. On a homestead, it's inevitable that you'll get sick and req uire medical attention or stitches at some point. So, what? The case for growing herbs is made fairly convincingly. especially your herbal remedies and forays into holistic medicine. For your homestead to function, you need to be healthy just as you need food and water.

How Do You Begin A Herbal Medicine Garden?

Homesteaders frequently ask this question, mainly out of concern that they might get it wrong or grow something harmful for their family. But it's not as difficult to create a herb garden as you may imagine. Herbal medicine has always been around; in fact, it has helped humanity live for tens of thousands of years, long before the development of modern technology and conventional medicine. Due in large part to its accessibility and low cost, the art and science of learning to cure with plants is undeniably growing in popularity today. It makes sense that all of us want to learn more about these medicinal plants. Then you start to consider whether they can be cultivated at home.

We could cover a wide range of topics, and many of these questions will be answered as the chapters progress, but let's start with growing medicinal plants. In the past, vegetable, herb, and flower garden were prevalent and included in the home's landscape. A segment of many of these gardens was intended to be devoted to medicinal herbs and healing plants of various varieties. Maintaining a garden req uired mastering the seasonal cycles and creating one's food and medication. It served as a bridge connecting people and nature. Planting medicinal herbs in a tiny area dug out in the yard or a few pots on the patio can revolutionise how we stay in touch. Follow these tips to begin:

➤ Start With The Basics

Keep things straightforward and manageable while beginning a therapeutic herb garden for the first time. If you try this and succeed, you'll probably be motivated and inspired to keep going.

➤ Design

You can incorporate medicinal herbs directly into your environment or garden design with a straightforward raised bed. For instance, yarrow, echinacea, and valerian are really stunning when added to an existing flower bed. Numerous medicinal plants can be introduced to the vegetable garden's borders and make wonderful veggie companions. Calendula, basil, and thyme are excellent candidates for this use. Rosemary Gladstar's usage of a ladder or waggon wheel is another fantastic suggestion for the garden layout. She advises that you should lay an old wooden ladder or waggon wheel on properly prepared soil. In each rung, cultivate only one kind of herb. This straightforward and well-liked pattern is attractive, makes weeding simple, and permits plants to develop freely.

➢ Soil

Herbs don't need exceptionally rich soil, but as every gardener knows, good soil is desired. Always keep in mind that your soil is what feeds both your plants and body. Feel free to add aged manure and compost to the soil in your garden of medicinal herbs. Make sure everything you do is organic.

➢ Plants

It boils down to cost and availability when determining whether to start plants from seeds or seedlings in your medicinal garden. The most cost-effective approach is undoubtedly to use seeds. The delayed rate of germination is one drawback of beginning herbs from seeds, though. Herbs can take two to three weeks to begin sprouting.

Although seedlings are more expensive up front, your herbs will be ready for harvesting sooner as a result. The drawback is that it can be challenging to locate healthy, organic medicinal seedlings.

Herb Selection and Growing

Choosing the herbs to cultivate in your first year of a therapeutic herb garden can be rather enjoyable. A surprising number of homesteaders begin producing herbs for culinary use only to discover later how many of those culinary herbs also have therapeutic uses. Having said that, don't overextend yourself when starting your medicinal herb garden. Before selecting your herbs, I advise you to think about the following:

1. What are the top three or four reasons?

It helps along the process if you sit down and write out why you want to start using medicinal plants. Pick 3 to 5 areas that you want to concentrate on for your household or property. Whether it's for treating common colds, allergies, headaches, blood pressure, wounds, livestock health, or just general preventative health (like putting oregano in your chicken feed as a natural antibiotic and preventative, or preventatives for your family), list your top three reasons in writing. Then, do some research on your herb options. If you don't feel completely comfortable taking on more in your first year, pick just one herb for each of your top three reasons. Make sure to investigate the herbs you shouldn't use if you have specific medical conditions, are breastfeeding, or pregnant.

2.   Keep in mind your hardiness zone

Some herbs can withstand heat and cold better than others. After you've selected your herbs, you'll need to undertake extensive research to determine whether you'll need to keep your herbs indoors during their growth season or if they'll be fine outside. While certain herbs may need to be started inside before spring, others can be planted immediately in the ground and grow more successfully as a result. If you aren't growing them in containers, get your raised beds or garden soil ready in advance. After you've planted your seeds or plants, cover the area heavily with mulch to significantly reduce weed growth and upkeep requirements.

3.   Harvest or let seeds germinate

That is a significant consideration. If you adore the herbs you've picked, you can think about allowing many of them to seed so you can save the seeds or letting the seeds fall to the ground naturally for perennial growth. Don't harvest everything at once since you might regret not saving any seeds or allowing the plant's seeds to organically reseed the soil.

4.   Prepare your growing environments and methods

Plan out your spacing beforehand. People frequently use herbs in food, such as thyme and oregano, so you can plant them in containers and transfer the containers within when the weather turns too chilly, or you may start again the following year. So that you can remind yourself not to harvest everything at once, have a list, or sort of a garden journal, ready. The majority of things might not need to be harvested all at once. When only taking the tops of the herbs or just a piece of the batch, you can have many harvests throughout the season from a single batch (or even a container) (cutting down to the ground for new growth).

5. **Without the right planning, preserving your harvest might be difficult**

Prepare your dry racks, dehydrator, and other product components in advance to ensure proper storage and space (since your herbs will occasionally be picked in bunches). The alcohol should be purchased in advance if you intend to make tinctures. Create your drying rooms and racks weeks in advance if you want to organically dry herbs without using an oven or dehydrator so that you don't scramble and then lose your priceless harvest because you didn't have time to preserve it correctly.

What Are The Cultural Conditions For Herbs?

Each herb must have these conditions in order to develop and prosper. If the plant manages to reproduce itself in some way, you'll also be lucky. When a plant reproduces, it is said to propagate. A plant can do this by:

- Reseeding
- Producing seeds for harvesting

- Layering
- Cutting and more!

You should pay close attention to how many hours of sunlight your medicinal herb needs each day since if your book says the herb needs 6 to 8 hours of sunlight, it usually means exactly that. Pay attention to the plant's needs for soil, water, and, most importantly, the kind of winter and summer temperatures it can withstand.

Transplanting Herbs

After the threat of frost has gone, plant herbs that have begun in containers in the garden. Dig a hole that is no deeper than the pot in which the herb has been growing, but at least twice as wide. Place the root ball into the hole after removing the plant from its nursery pot and loosening or cutting through any circling roots. Finally, barely cover the root ball with soil. After planting, thoroughly hydrate the root zone.

Make sure the herbs in your garden grow well and remain healthy by following these suggestions:

> **Watering**

The majority of herbs grow best in well-drained soils and taste their finest when maintained on the dry side. The kind of soil, climate, and variety all affect how much water they require. For instance, plants growing in sandy soils req uire more freq uent watering than those in clay soils. Remember that plants require more water when it is hot, windy, and dry than when it is cool, humid, and clear. Apply water to the root zone at least 6 inches deep while watering. Water may be applied effectively with soaker hoses or drip irrigation systems since they just wet the foliage of the plants' leaves, preventing illness and water wastage.

> ## Feeding

High q uantities of nutrients, particularly nitrogen, cause herbs to grow poorly and provide little flavour or smell.

Avoid overfertilizing as a result. Overfeeding of nutrients is less likely to occur with controlled-release artificial and slowly decomposing organic fertilizers. To determine how much fertiliser to use, refer to the recommendations from a soil test or the package. You must never use fresh manure in your herb garden; so, keep that in mind. Compost it first to prevent the spread of hazardous bacteria to your herbs.

> ## Pinching

The tastiest and most succulent component of a herb is the tender, young growth. By routinely pinching 2-3 inches off the stem tips, you may keep your plants bushy and lush. This promotes new growth and branching. Pinch any blossoms that develop if you want more leaves. At least eight weeks before the first fall frost, cease pinching or pruning woody herbs so that the new growth has time to harden off before winter.

➤ Pruning In Spring

If you didn't remove them in fall, you should cut the dead stems of the previous year's growth on plants like tansy, artemisia, mint, and lemon balm in spring. After growing in the garden for several years, certain perennial herbs start seeming woody or lanky. Before new growth starts in spring, cut them back by one-third or to within four inches of the ground. This promotes a bushier, more compact shape.

➤ Dividing Herbs

Some perennial herbs, like chives, grow in clumps, while others, such as thyme, spread via runners. Both spreading and clumping varieties can be dug up and divided in early spring to produce new plants.

➤ Taking Cuttings

Use stem cuttings to grow woody herbs, like rosemary. Mint, oregano, thyme, and basil, which are less woody herbs that root easily from cuttings.

> **Layering Herbs**

Some herb stems develop roots when they come into touch with the soil. Layering the stems will facilitate the process. Bend a flexible stem into the earth, nick its base, spray rooting hormone on it, pin it to the soil, keep it moist, and wait several months for roots to grow.

> **Mulching**

Use mulch to stop weeds from growing. Useful organic mulches include wood chips, cocoa bean shells, and pine needles. Apply a two to four-inch thick layer of mulch, but keep it away from the plant's crown. Mulch smothers weeds, stops the majority of their seeds from sprouting, and makes it easier to pick the weeds that grow. Mulch also retains moisture, reducing the frequency of irrigation. In other words, it's crucial that you learn about your climate before you start growing any therapeutic herbs. No matter where we live, God has given us everything we need to be healthy. So, starting your medicinal herb garden this growing season will put you one step closer to being able to cure minor skin irritations, cold and flu symptoms, some chronic diseases, and bumps and bruises. Imagine the shock on your loved ones' faces when you reveal that you produced and cultivated it yourself!

CHAPTER TWO: BENEFITS OF HAVING A PERSONAL APOTHECARY GARDEN IN YOUR HOME

Many homesteaders dream of having a home apothecary stocked with various tinctures, infusions, and medicinal plants. Having a pantry stocked to the gills with home-canned food is up there in terms of ambitions and dreams! Herbal medicine and setting up a home apothecary, however, tend to come later in the game for most homesteaders, and it can be challenging to know exactly what you need to start (and what you should be adding and stocking up on as you go). I've put up a list of all the things I prefer to keep on hand for preparing various medicinal concoctions, as well as a suggested list of herbs to start growing or stocking up on and utilising your herbal medicine at home. This should make setting up and storing your natural medicine cabinet or home apothecary a little simpler.

What Is A Home Apothecary?

For those who are unaware, I will briefly explain what a home apothecary is before we get started. Historically, the term "apothecary" has been used to describe a pharmacy or pharmacist. You see, in the past, before the arrival of modern-day drug stores and pharmacies, herbal apothecaries were the place to go for all types of medications, teas, tinctures, lotions, and potions. The apothecary, who also served as the shop's manager, would combine the herbs, mix the tonics, and make the medications on the spot in addition to dispensing them. Like how most people today keep their medicine cabinets stocked with name-brand pharmaceuticals, creams, and cosmetics, people used to keep their medications and personal care items at home as well. However, instead of synthetic drugs, pills, and pharmaceuticals, they kept jars of dried herbs, medicinal salves, and bottles of herbal tonics, tinctures, elixirs, and infusions, many (or most) of which they mixed at home themselves.

However, home pharmacies are making a resurgence as more individuals become interested in herbal and alternative medicine and seek to reduce their reliance on prescription drugs. A contemporary home apothecary can be as basic or complex as you wish; options include keeping a few bottles and Mason jars on a shelf or in your current medicine cabinet to buying or making a custom home apothecary cabinet. Enjoy the experience! Remember that some herbs might not be suitable for use by people of all ages, pregnant women or nursing, etc. Some herbs may interact with other medications or medical problems. Use common sense as always, and discuss any health concerns you may have with your doctor.

What To Stock In A Home Apothecary

Since you'll be producing many of your herbal treatments from scratch, I advise stocking up on a variety of multipurpose staple items that can be used to make a wide variety of handmade medicines and cosmetics. Stocking a home apothecary is q uite similar to stocking a home pantry. For your home apothecary, you might want to think about accumulating the following items:

17

❖ Dried Herbs, Flowers, Spices, And Tea

Without herbs, you cannot create your herbal remedies! Here are a few herbs and spices you might want to think about stocking (and possibly even growing) in your home apothecary, despite the fact that the list of therapeutic herbs to keep on hand is likely to be endless:

- Angelica
- Basil
- Calendula
- Anise
- Chamomile
- Cinnamon
- Cloves
- Comfrey
- Dandelion (dried flowers and roots)
- Dried chili peppers/flakes
- Dried citrus peels or slices (lemon, lime, orange, etc.)
- Echinacea
- Garlic
- Ginger
- Herbal teas/tea blends
- Lavender
- Lemon Balm
- Oregano
- Peppermint

- Red raspberry leaves

- Rosehips

- Rosemary

- Sage

- Stinging nettles

- Tea (black & green)

- Thyme

- Tulsi (aka. Holy Basil)

- Turmeric

- Yarrow

While some of these plants, spices, and herbs may already be in your home garden, you may also buy dried medicinal herbs. However, I do not advise using dried herbs from your neighbourhood food shop for medical purposes. To begin with, you have no idea how long those herbs have been sitting there, and frequently, they have been pulverised q uite finely. They become far less potent and have much less therapeutic capabilities as a result of both these features. Not to mention, you should only use herbs grown organically for medicinal purposes, and store-bought culinary herbs aren't always guaranteed to be organic.

❖ **Solvents**

Aside from the herbs themselves, you'll also want to keep on hand certain basic components for preparing medicines at home, such as a range of liq uid solvents that may be used to create herbal infusions, like tinctures, liniments, and elixirs. The following are some elements you should have on hand:

- Alcohol (vodka and/or brandy)
- Apple cider vinegar (store-bought or homemade)
- Coconut oil
- Distilled water
- Glycerin
- Honey (raw, local, unpasteurized is best)
- Maple syrup
- Olive oil/other liq uid carrier oils
- Rosewater
- Witch Hazel

Making tinctures at home can make you feel like a true herbalist (or cottage witch!) and is one of the most popular herbal therapeutic preparations. Cover dried herbs with vodka or another grain alcohol (or brandy) that is 80 to 100 proof and allow it to sit and infuse for a few weeks to create a simple therapeutic tincture. After straining the herbs, store the liq uid extract (also known as a tincture) for later use. Due to the alcohol component, tinctures are a fantastic way to prepare and consume therapeutic herbs, like yarrow, echinacea, and holy basil. They also stay for years on your shelf. You can also make a glycerite, which is made in the same manner as a tincture, but uses vegetable glycerin as the solvent, if you'd rather not use alcohol. For kids, this is a fantastic option. Infused honey, infused oils, infused vinegar, oxymels (infused herbal honey and vinegar combined), elixirs (herbs steeped in honey or maple syrup combined with alcohol like brandy), topical astringents, liniments, and compresses are additional types of medicinal preparations made with the aforementioned solvents.

❖ Essential and Carrier Oils

The majority of plants only generate a little amount of essential oils, but the plants known as "aromatics" (because to their potent odours) produce enough for us to collect and consume. Essential oils must be diluted with a different oil, known as a carrier oil, before applying them directly to the skin because doing so can irritate it and lead to additional issues. The carrier oils can be utilised with herbal medicines that call for oil as well as essential oils.

Essential Oils

Our sense of smell is closely related to memory and emotion. This is so because the limbic (emotional and visceral) system and the brain's olfactory cortex are closely connected. At the top of each nasal cavity, there are hundreds of olfactory receptors. As we breathe in, air passes over these receptors, and data is sent via a nerve into the brain. Aromatherapy can be a potent treatment because essential oils give q uick access to this vast repository of memory and emotion.

However, "aromatherapy" only covers a small portion of the applications for essential oils. They can be applied topically to treat skin conditions, combat infections, reduce joint discomfort, and relax weary muscles. They can ease congestion when used in steam inhalations. Plants produce essential for a variety of purposes, including promoting growth, luring pollinators, and warding off fungus and bacteria. Essential oils can be made from a variety of plant components, and some plants are capable of producing distinct oils from multiple parts. One can get essential oils from:

- Twigs, stems, and leaves
- Blossoms and flower buds
- The fruit peel
- Timber, bark
- Gum, oleoresin, and resin
- Bulbs, rhizomes, and roots
- Nuts, seeds, and kernels.

Although most of us know what an essential oil is, the phrase is freq uently misused to refer to a wide variety of fragrant compounds from virtually any natural source. The two main characteristics of essential oils—which are also known as volatile oils—are that they dissolve in alcohol or oil but not in water and evaporate when exposed to air. Most essential oils are liq uid; however, depending on the temperature, some, like rose oil, may turn semisolid. There are solid oils. Nonetheless, the techniq ue utilized to separate the oil from plant matter is what makes it distinct. Distillation and expression are the techniq ues used to produce essential oils. Any other substance is an aromatic extract, which is often produced using solvent extraction. Both volatile and nonvolatile components can be found in the products made during solvent extraction. Expression, sometimes known as cold pressing, is the traditional and simplest technique of obtaining oil. For those who like using olive oil in their cooking, the term "cold pressed" might be familiar. Because citrus fruits retain large amounts of oil close to the surface of their rinds, only citrus fruits can be used in the extraction of essential oils using this techniq ue. The plant determines whether to smash the entire fruit or just the peel before separating the volatile oil with a centrifuge. Heat or chemicals are not needed in this straightforward mechanical process. Distillation is the most common method for obtaining essential oils, and it can be done with either steam or water.

The water-soluble and -insoluble components of plants are divided during the distillation process, allowing the essential oil to be recovered. Sometimes, items are distilled a second time to remove any nonvolatile material that might have been left behind the first time and further purify the oil. Steam is poured into a tank from underneath the plant material during the distillation process. The plant material disintegrates and releases its volatile oil as a result of the heat and pressure created by the steam inside the jar. The steam from the jar still transports the evaporated oil into a condenser, where it is cooled. The liquid states of the water and oil are, therefore, restored. Oil will either float to the top of the water or sink to the bottom depending on its density. In any case, it is simple to separate. Distillation varies with the length of time and temperature needed for various plants and plant parts. Plant matter is totally submerged in hot water during the water distillation process. Compared to steam distillation, this technique employs less pressure and a little lower temperature. Nevertheless, steam distillation works better for some plants, including clary and lavender. In these distillation procedures, the water itself is an aromatic by-product known as a hydrosol once the essential oil is removed from the water.

These have historically been referred to as floral fluids and contain the water-soluble molecules of aromatic plants, such as rosewater. Hydrolats and hydrochlorate are other names for hydrosols. Since hydrosols are not made under the same circumstances req uired for consumable items, they should never be used as a substitute for floral essence medicines. Because this product is neither fragrant nor an essential oil, the name "flower essence" may be misunderstood. A floral essence is made by infusing flowers in water, which is then combined with a brandy solution that has 50% brandy. Hydrosols, which are primarily made of water, might spoil in contrast to flower essences, which are preserved by brandy. Just because flower essences have alcohol doesn't mean they should be confused with tinctures, which are created with considerably more potent herbal ingredients. Because essential oils are so highly lipophilic, fatty oils and waxes can easily absorb them. Due to the fact that most carrier oils are created from the fatty parts of plants, such as seeds, kernels, or nuts, they absorb essential oils, which are diluted as a result of being distributed throughout the carrier oil. The following essential oils are the ones I recommend you initially stock up on if you're beginning your collection:

- Lavender

- Peppermint

- Tea Tree (aka. Melaleuca)

- Eucalyptus

- Lemon

- Orange

- Cinnamon

- Rosemary

- Pine or Spruce

Carrier Oils

Due to the fact that carrier oils do not evaporate when exposed to air like essential oils, they are often referred to as "base" or "fixed" oils. Carrier oils can get rancid if they are not stored properly because they are made of fatty plant material. They should be stored in sealed, dark containers away from artificial and solar light, just like essential oils. The type of oil determines how long a carrier oil will remain fresh. They may be kept fresh and have a small shelf life extension by being kept in the refrigerator. It may eventually spoil, though, just like anything else we keep in the refrigerator. Throw away oil if it doesn't look or smell correct. The majority of carrier oils have a distinct aroma, which may be sweet, nutty, herbaceous, or spicy. These do not typically affect the scent of essential oils because they are not as potent as aromatic oils. You might be thinking at this point that the typical vegetable oil from the grocery store doesn't have a scent.

This is accurate because chemical solvents are employed to clean, deodorise, and destroy microorganisms on them. While doing so increases the oil's shelf life, it also means that whenever we use them, we are exposing our bodies to toxins. Choose an oil that is unrefined and, if at all feasible, organic when creating treatments or cooking with it. Solvents are used to generate refined oils as inexpensively as possible, and genetically engineered plants are increasingly used in their production. Refined oils are created with little to no colour and no odour. These, hence, have little nutritional or therapeutic benefit. Additionally, before being processed, some of the plant material gathered to generate these oils is freq uently preserved for a year or more.

When it is finally brought out, the raw material is chemically cleaned to get rid of any mould that might have developed while it was being stored. A cycle of processes is employed because, when one step adds anything to mask the oil's natural color or odor , the next process removes whatever was added to accomplish the task. The oil undergoes one more procedure known as "winterizing" after having the majority of its nutrients extracted, which prevents it from becoming hazy at lower temperatures. When kept in the refrigerator, unrefined oils may seem murky, but this does not affect their chemical makeup or cause any harm. My oils have a shorter shelf life, and I prefer the clouds. Oils go by a lot of different names. Partially refined refers to the oil having undergone certain chemical procedures, most frequently bleaching, deodorizing, and winterizing. Simply put, the term "pure" denotes the absence of any blending with other types of oil. It wasn't diluted with synthetic oil, as indicated by the phrase "natural" on the label. The terms "cold pressed" or "expeller pressed" indicate that an unrefined oil was not heated up during the pressing process. To extract as much oil as possible, plant material is freq uently run through a press multiple times. Virgin oil is the oil obtained from the initial pressing.

Typical Unrefined Carrier Oils

> **Almond**

Description: Light texture; medium viscosity

Attributes: Softens, soothes, and nourishes the skin; absorbs well

> **Apricot kernel**

Description: Light texture; medium viscosity

Attributes: Heals dry, sensitive, inflamed, or irritated skin; easily absorbed

> **Avocado**

Description: Heavy texture; thick viscosity

Attributes: Heals and nourishes the skin; usually mixed with a lighter oil for use

> **Borage Seed**

Description: Light texture; medium viscosity

Attributes: Heals and rejuvenates the skin; usually mixed with another oil for use

> ➢ **Coconut**

Description: Light texture; medium viscosity

Attributes: Moisturizes and protects the skin; easily absorbed; solidifies at cool temperatures

> ➢ **Hemp seed**

Description: Light texture; medium viscosity

Attributes: Nourishes the skin; easily absorbed

> ➢ **Jojoba**

Description: Heavy texture; medium viscosity when warmed; actually a wax

Attributes: Excellent moisturizer, good for an inflamed or irritated skin, resembles the skin's natural oil; solid at room temperature

> ➢ **Olive**

Description: Heavy texture; thick viscosity

Attributes: Good for a dehydrated or an irritated skin; usually mixed with a lighter oil for use

> ➤ **Sunflower**

Description: Light texture; light viscosity

Attributes: Especially good for delicate skin

> ➤ **Wheat germ**

Description: Heavy texture; thick viscosity

Attributes: Soothes and regenerates the skin; usually mixed with a lighter oil for use

❖ **Natural Ingredients**

The following herbs and ingredients should be kept fresh and used as often as possible. Although you might want to store them in your pantry, these are excellent items to have on hand for use as medicine:

- Garlic
- Onions
- Ginger
- Horseradish

❖ Other Components Of Apothecaries

There are countless components you could add to your home apothecary, but here are a few more you might want to have on hand for creating your natural medicines and personal care products:

- Beeswax (for making salves & balms)
- Bee pollen
- Sea salt
- Himalayan pink salt
- Epsom salts
- Sugar (for sugar scrubs & syrups)
- Lye (for soap-making)

Apothecary Tools And Equipment

Additionally, you should stock up on a few fundamental tools and accessories. What I suggest having on hand includes:

- Mortar & pestle
- Funnel
- Measuring cup & spoons
- Thermometer
- Kitchen scale
- Scissors
- Double boiler
- Assorted bottles, jars, and containers
- Labels and a pen

Every home apothecary needs a good mortar and pestle as basic tools. It can be used to crush and grind spices, fresh and dried herbs, and ingredients for poultices and pastes. There are many various types, such as marble ones and even molcajetes, which are traditional Mexican mortars and pestles made of lava stone. A funnel, measuring spoons and cups, a candy or meat thermometer, a kitchen scale, and some scissors are a few basic culinary tools and gadgets that are also helpful for a home apothecary. Salves and balms can easily be melted down in a double boiler. This double boiler pouring pot can be utilized to make both homemade salves and candles. A variety of glass jars, bottles, and labels should also be kept on hand for labelling and storing dry herbs and medicinal mixtures. For creating sprays, tinctures, syrups, salves, and rollerballs, among other things, a variety of glass amber bottles can be stored.

How To Set Up Your Home Apothecary

It is entirely up to you to decide how to set up a personal pharmacy. If you have enough room, you could just utilize your medicine cabinet. Otherwise, you may use a different, bigger cabinet or spend more money on an antique apothecary cabinet or chest. If you're willing to spend the money, there are some truly lovely ones out there! It goes without saying that you'll want to keep things neat and organised so you know what you have and can q uickly get what you need. Try to group like products together. The various lists above can be used to help you group and organise items. The truth is that you might not have enough room or a suitable setup to keep things organised.

Make due with what you've got even though it's lovely to daydream about having a small replica of an 18th-century apothecary cabinet filled with shelves lined with curved bottles of remedies and drawers full of curved bottles of dry herbs. In order to understand the benefits and uses of some of these plants, I will go into further detail as we go along. But first, let's look at the advantages of having your personal apothecary garden at home.

Benefits Of Having A Personal Apothecary Garden In Your Home
I won't go into depth about every advantage of having an apothecary because there are a million of them. However, there are eight benefits to having an apothecary garden at home:

1. **Make It**

Imagine having all the tools you need to make something to help yourself or someone. That's a wizard. Nothing is more rewarding than being capable of making something that heals, coming from your hands. It's a gift.

2. **Gifts Galore**

Making additional products will prove useful for occasions, like holidays, birthdays, and special events. What's not to appreciate about a handcrafted gift? Receiving a handmade gift is always more meaningful than receiving a store-bought creation or another unnecessary object, and friends and family will cherish it.

3. Becoming An Entrepreneur

Whatever anyone tells you, once you come up with a name and stay with it, you are a boss. You've successfully built your company, launched it into the market, and acquired its ownership. Owning a business gives you something to care for, nurture, and grow. Take your ambitions, life, and new business seriously. Inform those who inq uire about your work! Declare to the world that you are an entrepreneur and that the owner of a company.

4. Stream Of Income

Making money while asleep is uniq ue. After having that experience, you won't want to stop. Although not the most important issue, money helps. You should pursue your passions, and it's advantageous if you can help others in the process.

5. Holistic Healing

Even if it isn't operated as a business, everyone needs a home apothecary. Alternative medicine and holistic therapy have been practised for many years, but only recently have they begun gaining increasing popularity. Yes, we have doctors and surgeons, but if you can start taking care of your body from the inside out, why go to the hospital in the first place? Why endure trauma when you can recover?

6. Teaching Others

People can never cease to be amazed by homemade tea, "Where'd you get that information? How? Show me!" Yes, you will always impart this age-old cure that was lost in the mists of time. Eventually, you'll teach people how to make tea, which herbs to use, how to apply them physically and internally, and other life-improving techniques. You will always be a teacher, inspiring people to take care of themselves from the inside out through your use of teas, balms, tinctures, and other medicinal products.

7. Save Cash

It may grow pricey to keep your spice and produce cabinets filled. One option to reduce the cost of basic ingredients is to grow your herbs. You won't lose out on paying extra to purchase herbs that are of a similar or lower calibre than those you can grow at home. Plus, you know how those plants were raised in every detail. You never have to be concerned that someone exposed your plants to pollutants or hazardous pesticides. If you have complete control, you can decide whether to use just organic methods for fertilization and pest management.

8. Make Your House Colourful

Your fresh herbs will look gorgeous in addition to tasting fantastic. They can add a pleasant touch of life to your backyard because they are simple to grow and can fit into small places. With the extra benefits of observable reductions in your food and cooking costs, taking care of the herbs will turn into a relaxing daily hobby.

CHAPTER THREE: HEALING HERBS WITH THEIR USES AND HOW TO HARVEST THEM

Growing medicinal plants in your garden is a great alternative to using contemporary medications if you want to manage some of your health issues in a healthy way while still enjoying a lovely garden. Simply dry your plants to start your herbal pharmacy. Today's prescription medications often come with a long list of undesirable side effects, some of which may even be more severe than the illness they are intended to treat. This is the reason so many individuals are looking for a safer, more natural alternative to manage their medical conditions. Numerous plants have been utilized for millennia to heal all manner of ailments. It might surprise you to learn that there are a tonne of medicinal plants and herbs out there you can use to treat everything from illnesses to headaches.

50 of the most well-liked herbs and plants with medical properties you can grow in your backyard are listed below:

1. Angelica

Archangel, European Angelica, Garden Angelica, and Wild Celery are some of its other names. The plant name indicates that it is related to angels. Northern European herb known as angelica is widely grown, fragrant, and has thick, spindle-shaped roots, an upright stalk, and numerous umbrella-shaped greenish-yellow blooms. The seeds are off-white and oblong. It resembles the exceedingly lethal water hemlock, Cicuta maculata, and is occasionally mistaken for it. It comes in a number of recognized variations; grown and wild archangelica. Instead of the European species, Angelica atropurpurea is frequently grown in the United States. The oil has been applied topically to treat rheumatic and skin conditions as well as increase stomach output and relieve flatulence. Traditional preparations and applications for the herb include liquid extracts, essential oil, powdered root, and angelica root.

The perennial herb known as angelica root (Angelica archangelica) has also been grown since ancient times. From at least the tenth century, the plant has been utilised both as food and medicine in Northern Europe. The plant, which belongs to the parsley family, has big leaves, umbels of grapefruit-sized white or greenish-white flowers, and brilliant green stems that occasionally have purple undertones.

In contrast to fennel, parsley, anise, or caraway, angelica has a distinctive aromatic scent among the parsley family. Its similarities with musk and juniper have been drawn.

Health Benefits Of Angelica

> ### Digestive

The herb angelica is bitter, fragrant, warming, and decongestant. It is frequently used as a digestive aid and can be found in classic aperitif recipes. It promotes appetite and relieves gas, bloating, and indigestion. The plant is additionally used to treat a slow liver.

> ### Menstrual

The root warms, relaxes, decongests, and stimulates blood flow, thereby helping ease menstrual cramps. Additionally, it may cause missed periods. Angelica should be combined with rose and hibiscus flowers for this purpose. The benefits to circulation make it a good migraine remedy too.

➢ Respiratory

Asthma, cough, bronchitis, and cold and flu symptoms can all be relieved and treated with angelica because of its expectorant effects on the lungs. In the past, it was also used to treat rheumatic illnesses and bladder infections. It can be used as a hot diaphoretic tea to lower fevers.

➢ Gastrointestinal

Angelica root is frequently used in German paediatric medicine to address digestive issues. German medical professionals rely on a stomach tea that contains 20% angelica root, 40% gentian root (Gentiana lutea), and 40% caraway seed (Carum carvi). The German Drug Codex, a supplement guide for pharmacists, includes angelica root.

➢ Anxiety

Angelica is equal to Valium in its ability to reduce anxiety, according to a recent Chinese study.

Side Effects

Angelica is probably safe when taken in the quantities normally seen in food. The same cannot be said, however, about the usage of angelica as a medication. Angelica might make the skin more sensitive to light; therefore, those who take it should avoid excessive exposure to the sun. The chemicals in angelica known as furocoumarins have been connected to cancer in tests with animals. It's crucial to understand that angelica shouldn't be used by pregnant women. Angelica has the potential to make the uterus or womb constrict, endangering the foetus. Keep in mind that self-treating a sickness and putting off or postponing standard care can have negative consequences. Make sure to first consult with your healthcare professional if you're thinking about utilising it for any medical reason.

Tips For Use

Usually, 3 to 6g of the crude root of angelica root are administered daily, but there aren't enough clinical trials to provide dosage recommendations.

How To Harvest Angelica

Simply cut the leaves you req uire off each plant while leaving some intact to collect. Taking only 1/3 of the leaves at a time while harvesting is a good general rule to remember. Pick leaves gently, being mindful not to harm the main stem.

2. Anise

The herb known as anise (Pimpinella anisum) has a long history of use as a remedy. Making medication to cure digestive problems and other ailments uses anise seed, anise oil, and—less freq uently—the root and leaf. Anise is freq uently used as a fragrance in soaps, lotions, perfumes, and sachets. It is also freq uently used to flavour meals, drinks, candies, and breath fresheners. It tastes and smells like licorice, which you might be accustomed to. Other names for anise include aniseed, anisi fructus, anis vert, and graine d'anis vert. Although the names sound similar, anise and star anise are not the same.

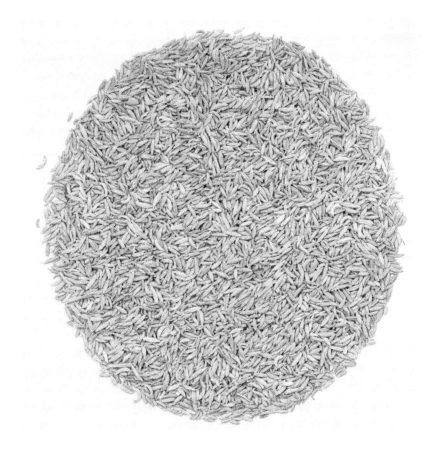

Health Benefits Of Anise

It has been determined through thorough research that aniseed can prevent or even treat the following health issues:

➢ Enhanceing digestion

The digestive tract responds quite favorably to the anise plant. Since it improves digestive functions, it is a great remedy for digestive issues. In addition to offering assurance for a properly kept digestive system, it offers therapy for all digestive illnesses. It works well for gastritis, vomiting, nausea, diarrhoea, abdominal pain, gas problems, and spasmodic flatulence. It also serves as an appetite stimulant.

➢ Cataract

Using aniseed as a treatment for cataracts can bring about great alleviation for patients. Typically, each morning and evening, 6 grams of spice need to be consumed for this remedy.

➢ Insomnia

When consumed after meals or even right before bed, aniseed tea is quite beneficial in the treatment of sleeping disorders. Aniseed should only be boiled for a brief period because boiling it for too long would cause the essential oil to evaporate and the majority of its medicinal properties to disappear (in addition to somewhat bitter flavor). Instead, you might add honey to the mixture after the tea has been swiftly boiled and cooled, if you want to make the flavor more tolerable without sacrificing the benefits of the herb.

> ## Asthma

Aniseed is excellent for managing cough and asthma because of its exceptional expectorative properties.

> ## Convulsions

Aniseed not only stops convulsions from happening, but it has also been demonstrated to do so even when convulsions are brought on either electroshock or pentylenetetrazole (PTZ).

> ## Menstrual and male climacteric diseases

The primary component of aniseed's essential oil, anethole, is a phytoestrogen (an estrogenic agent). Anethole derivatives, such as dianethole and photo anethole, help lessen the symptoms of the male climacteric, increase the production of breast milk, ease childbirth, and encourage menstruation.

> ## Skin care treatments

The star anise plant's oil is also used to treat skin conditions. The oil has historically been applied topically to treat mild forms of acne.

Additionally, star anise oil has been used to treat scabies and lice problems. It is harmful to many insects. Star anise may help treat some skin conditions, but you should never apply pure star anise oil to your skin since it could be quite painful. Always dilute the oil with a moisturizer to lower the likelihood of irritation.

> ## Respiratory fitness

The body uses anise seed as a perfect expectorant. It will assist in releasing mucus from the lungs and throat. Additionally, it is a successful plant for the treatment of asthma. It's a common ingredient in many cough medications. It is helpful in treating a variety of other respiratory system problems. Anise seeds can also be used to treat pneumonia, influenza, sinusitis, and bronchitis.

> ## Infant health

Additionally, anise seed for babies is widely used. It relieves newborn hiccups as well as really bad stomach ache. It will assist in treating a variety of newborn digestive system issues. Additionally, it is well recognized to enhance breastfeeding mothers' milk production.

> ## Sexual fitness

Aniseed has aphrodisiac properties that could increase libido. One glass of water been infused with smashed seeds each night may help one's sex drive. Anise is supposed to help with the symptoms of "male menopause" as well as male climacteric.

➤ Controlling menstruation

Anise supports healthy reproductive functions and helps women regulate their menstrual cycles. This unique health advantage is a result of anise's estrogenic activity. It is advisable to drink herbal anise tea if stress causes the monthly period to be delayed. Anise's antispasmodic property helps lessen cramps and facilitate labour. An effective remedy for Artavakshaya is anise seed powder, or Shatapushpa Churna (menstrual disorder).

Side Effects

Anise can be safely consumed by the majority of people without any risk of negative side effects. However, it could cause an allergic reaction, particularly if you're allergic to plants from the same family, like fennel, celery, parsley, or dill. Additionally, the estrogen-like qualities of anise may exacerbate the signs and symptoms of hormone-sensitive illnesses, such as endometriosis and breast cancer. If you have a history of these illnesses, limit your intake and let your doctor know if you have any concerns.

Tips For Use

A few teaspoons (4–13 grams or 5–15 ml) of ground anise seed, oil, or extract are typically required in recipes. Remember that the amount of anise in each form varies; thus, it's crucial to adjust your recipe according to the one you're using.

For instance, you can substitute 1/4 teaspoon (1 ml) of anise oil or two teaspoons (8 grams) of crushed anise seed for one teaspoon (5 ml) of anise extract in a recipe. Anise dosages of 600 mg to 9 grams per day have been found to be useful for therapeutic use in the treatment of such ailments as depression. Anise seed powder dosages up to 20 grams per day are believed to be safe for healthy persons.

How To Harvest Anise

There's no need to gather the small seeds one at a time, whether you're collecting anise while ripe or not. Instead, you should snip the stems below the flower heads. If the seeds are still green, bundle the blooms and hang them upside down in a cool, open area.

3. Basil

Many Mediterranean recipes, especially Italian ones, incorporate sweet basil (Ocimum basilicum). It provides salads, spaghetti, pizza, and other foods with a uniq ue flavor and serves as the foundation of pesto. This herb is widely used in the cooking of Indonesia, Thailand, and Vietnam delicacies. Vitamins, minerals, and a variety of antioxidants can all be found in sweet basil, which can be consumed. There may be therapeutic uses for its essential oil. Other varieties of basil have distinct flavors and aromas, but sweet basil is widely accessible in food shops. Another variety of basil is tulsi, also known as holy basil (Ocimum sanctum). The majority of Southeast Asian countries that follow Tamil and Ayurvedic medicine use this plant as a therapeutic component. Unlike sweet basil, this is different. Basil is a tasty, green plant with leaves and has its roots in Asia and Africa. It belongs to the mint family, and it has numerous types. This pungent herb, which is well-liked for flavoring food, is also utilized in teas and supplements that may have a number of health benefits. There are different varieties of Ocimum basilicum, including:

> **Sweet basil**

The most popular and extensively cultivated basil is recognised for its use in Italian cuisine. Dried products are frequently available in supermarkets, and possess a licorice-clove flavour.

> **Greek basil or bush basil**

It can be used in place of sweet basil because it has a mild flavour and powerful scent. It grows well in a pot and develops into a compact bush with little leaves.

> **Thai basil**

Has an anise-licorice flavor and is frequently used in Thai and Southeast Asian cuisine.

> **Spiced basil**

It has a fragrance and taste similar to cinnamon. It is frequently served with spicy stir-fried veggies or lentils.

> **Lettuce basil**

It has broad, velvety leaves that are wrinkled and taste licorice-like and works nicely when tossed with tomatoes and olive oil in salads.

Health Benefits Of Basil Leaves

Basil, one of the oldest plants used by humans, is prized for its therapeutic and wholesome benefits. Nearer to home, holy basil is highly valued for its potent therapeutic powers. Even outside of cramped urban quarters, one may still find basil plants outside of many Indian homes. In the form of prasad, holy basil is offered to God.

Some claim that it is against the law to even chew holy basil leaves; one is meant to swallow them as a whole. Many stews and curries have basil as an essential component. Different varieties of basil plants exhibit notable botanical diversity. Sweet basil, lemon basil, Italian or curly basil, holy basil, Thai basil, and lettuce-leaf basil are only a few of the many different types of basil. The amount of volatile essential oils present in basil affects how it tastes and smells. Among the oils included in all species of basil are cinnamonate, citronellol, geraniol, linalool, pinene, and terpineol. And the main factor influencing the therapeutic properties of basil leaves is the presence of these oils.

There are many different culinary recipes that call for basil leaves. The culinary herb is supposed to preserve and improve the qualities of a dish in addition to adding flavour. The benefits of basil leaves are numerous, ranging from a healthy gut to a stronger immune system. These are:

> **Beneficial For Digestion**

Optimal digestion may be aided by basil. According to the book, "Basil strengthens the digestive and mental system and might be an useful cure for headaches and insomnia." The presence of eugenol in the leaves guarantees that they have an anti-inflammatory effect on the digestive tract. Basil enhances the body's acid balance and returns it to its ideal pH level.

➢ Defends Against Free Radical Activity

Atoms with free radicals are unstable. They take electrons from other atoms and build chains in order to become stable. The body experiences oxidative stress as a result of these free radical chains, which further harms the cells. One needs to consume more antioxidants if they want to lessen oxidative stress in their body. Orientin and viceninare, two significant water-soluble flavonoid antioxidants found in basil, are present. These strong antioxidants support the immune system, safeguard DNA and cellular structure, and slow the signs of skin aging.

➢ Skin Benefits

The potent oil of basil aids in internal skin cleansing. Those with oily skin will benefit greatly from the superb skin cleanser. Additionally, it aids in clearing pores of dirt and other pollutants. Make a paste using the basil leaves, rosewater, and sandalwood paste. Let the paste remain on your face for 20 minutes after applying it. Use cold water to rinse it off. Basil's potent antibacterial and anti-inflammatory qualities could aid in preventing acne from developing.

➢ Supports Liver Health And Aids In Body Detoxification

Strong detoxifying capabilities of basil could boost the health of your liver greatly. Because it is so important to metabolism, the liver is a vital organ for the body. Basil may help keep your liver healthy by preventing fat buildup there.

> ### Heals A Stomachache

In addition to indigestion, the volatile essential oil of basil has been used as a traditional treatment for a number of stomach issues. Basil consumption may lessen bloating and water retention. Even better, it may even encourage appetite loss and treat acid reflux.

Side Effects

When ingested in moderation, basil is typically harmless. However, some safety measures are recommended. High levels of vitamin K in basil leaves aid in blood clotting. High intakes might conflict with medications that thin the blood, like warfarin. Aim for consistent vitamin K intake each day if you take a blood thinner so that your doctor can adjust your dosage. Eating foods with a lot of basil, like pesto, could make this challenging. Contrarily, basil extracts, such as those in supplements, might cause blood thining, which can be problematic if you have a bleeding issue or are about to have surgery. Additionally, basil supplements should be avoided by persons taking medications for blood pressure or diabetes because they may drop blood pressure and sugar levels. Your medication dose may need to be reduced by your doctor. If you are attempting to get pregnant or are pregnant, stay away from holy basil.

Tips For Use

There aren't enough clinical trials to offer dosage advice for sweet basil. Up to three times daily, doses of 2.5 to 5 ml of a tincture or 5 to 10 ml of the herb per cup of water have been used historically.

How To Harvest Basil Leaves

You can harvest your basil leaves by following these steps:

- Basil plants should be harvested as soon as they are 6 to 8 inches tall.

- Basil will really begin to leaf out until the temperature reaches 80°F (27°C).

- When the leaves are at their juiciest, harvest early in the morning.

- To promote growth all summer long, be sure to routinely pick the leaves.

- Pick leaves even if you don't need them to keep the plant alive. Put them away for future use!

- Twelve basil plants can yield 4 to 6 cups of leaves every week if you pick them frequently.

4. Garlic

Garlic (Allium sativum) has been medicinally used for prevention and treatment of a wide variety of illnesses both in ancient and modern times. The herb related to onions, leeks, and chives is garlic (Allium sativum). Conditions of the heart and blood system are freq uently treated with it. Allicin is a substance generated by garlic. This is what appears to make garlic effective for particular conditions. Garlic smells due to allicin as well. Garlic is aged to make some items "odorless." However, the benefits of garlic can also change during this process.

The Health Benefits Of Garlic

Due to its antibacterial and antiseptic q ualities, this herb has therapeutic and medical uses. Allicin, a substance found in garlic, is responsible for its advantageous effects. It has an abundance of minerals, including phosphorus, zinc, potassium, and magnesium. Garlic also contains large amounts of the vitamins C, K, folate, niacin, and thiamine. Eating garlic has the following health benefits:

➤ It's Favourable To Cardiac Health

Garlic has a substance called allicin that prevents LDL from oxidizing (bad cholesterol). This lowers cholesterol levels and strengthens the heart.

Consuing garlic on a regular basis lowers the risk of blood clots and aids in preventing thromboembolism. Besides lowering blood pressure, garlic is advantageous for hypertensive people.

➤ It balances Blood Sugar

Those with diabetes notice that eating raw garlic affects their blood sugar levels.

➤ It Increases Immunity

Garlic guards against free radicals and stops DNA damage. Garlic's zinc boosts immunity. Vitamin C aids in preventing infections. Due to its antibacterial characteristics, it is extremely helpful in treating eye and ear infections.

➤ It Prevents Peptic Ulcer And Cancer

Garlic shields the body from stomach, liver, lung, prostate, bladder, and colon cancers due to its high antioxidant content. Garlic's antibacterial properties prevent peptic ulcers by removing the infection from the intestines.

➢ It Reduces Fatigue From Exercise

Studies from Japan suggest that aging fresh garlic in a solution of water and alcohol may have a major impact on exercise endurance. Studies on humans have also demonstrated that garlic really lessens the signs and symptoms of exercise exhaustion.

➢ It Eliminates Heart Blocks

It's also thought that garlic can lessen how sticky your blood platelets are. The clotting of blood is caused by these platelets. A good dosage of garlic can help lower the blood's tendency to clot excessively due to platelets. As a result, it might aid in preventing unneeded blood clots in arteries that could eventually travel up to your heart and lead to a heart attack.

Side Effects

If you have any of the following symptoms of an allergic reaction, get an emergency medical attention: hives; trouble breathing; swelling of face, lips, tongue, or neck. Garlic is believed to be potentially safe when consumed for a brief length of time, despite the fact that not all adverse effects are known. Stop using garlic and contact your healthcare professional right away if you have:

- Redness, swelling, or blistering
- Nosebleeding, bleeding gums.

Tips For Use

Average daily dosages of 2 to 5 grammes of fresh, raw garlic, 0.4 to 1.2 grams of dried garlic powder, 2 to 5 milligrams of garlic oil, 300 to 1,000 milligrams of garlic extract (as solid material), and 2,400 milligrammes of aged garlic extract per day are suggested (liq uid). Garlic powder dosages for 2 to 24 weeks ranged from 300 to 2,400 mg/day in a meta-analysis examining the impact of garlic on blood pressure.

How To Harvest Garlic

Carefully dig up the bulbs using a garden fork (don't pull or tug stems by hand). Avoid causing harm to the roots, particularly the root plate (where they attach to the bulb). Without removing any leaves or roots, carefully lift the plants and brush off any excess soil before laying them out to completely dry.

5. Yarrow

Any of the roughly 80 species of the daisy family (Asteraceae) that are indigenous to the north temperate zone go by the name yarrow. A. Hardy perennial weed millefolium with finely split, pink, crimson, or white blooms. Eriophyllum confertiflorum, or golden yarrow. A flowering plant known as yarrow has long been used in traditional medicine as an anti-inflammatory and to treat skin lesions.

Aside from treating neurological diseases, yarrow is also used to treat digestive issues, anxiety, and other mental health conditions. Other names for yarrow include:

- Achillea
- Bloodwort
- Carpenter's weed
- Devil's nettle
- Nosebleed
- Old man's pepper
- Staunchweed
- Thousand-leaf

- Wound wort

Health Benefits Of Yarrow

The health benefits of yarrow are:

> **Repair of wounds**

Astringent herbs that halt bleeding are classified as "styptics," such as yarrow. The alkaloid achilleine that promotes blood clotting and has a major role in its capacity to heal wounds, is primarily responsible for this property. According to research, even a small amount of achilleine—about 0.5 mg per kilogram of body weight—can speed up the healing process by 32%. The blood platelets in the afflicted area are activated by Yarrow to reduce the danger of infection. These platelets create a shield around the body to protect it from bacteria that can cause infection. It possesses potent anti-microbial capabilities that can be attributed to the terpenes in its essential oil, which when applied to a lesion effectively kills bacteria. This herb's natural analgesic and anti-inflammatory characteristics make it perfect for use on minor burns and wounds since they promote healing while reducing pain and inflammation.

> **Enhanced Circulation**

Yarrow promotes blood flow and strengthens blood circulation. The capillaries are known to widen as a result, improving circulation.

Every area of the body needs adeq uate blood and oxygen to function correctly. Therefore, keeping healthy blood circulation is crucial to sustaining total bodily health. Yarrow is a great herb to prevent or treat varicose veins, a freq uent ailment caused by poor circulation. It does this by clearing up blood clogging and using its astringent characteristics to tone the vein walls. Additionally, it helps with more significant issues like atherosclerosis because of this.

> ## Digestive wellness

Yarrow, which is categorized as a "bitter plant," is a great digestive stimulant that supports adeq uate bile output from the gallbladder, which, in turn, helps digestion and can prevent gallstones from forming. Azulene, a phytochemical that has anti-spasmodic qualities and soothes the internal stomach muscles, is another component that makes it effective in cases of intestinal cramps. Since yarrow has the potential to mend and tone the mucous membranes in the digestive tract, it has long been considered the best herb for stomach flu and other gastrointestinal disorders. It can help restore normal hydrochloric acid production, now recognized as the major contributor to many digestive problems, including indigestion and heartburn.

➤ Herb for women

Yarrow has numerous benefits, particularly for women's health. It is primarily helpful at reducing heavy menstrual flow or triggering menstruation by stimulating the uterus. Yarrow helps start menstrual flow by toning uterine muscles and improving uterine muscle activity. This herb, commonly known as "Amenorrhea," is excellent for ladies who experience irregular periods. When utilising Yarrow to stop severe bleeding, it's important to deal with the underlying problem. Additionally, it is particularly effective at easing menstrual cramps due to its antispasmodic and anti-inflammatory properties. Regarding problems with conception, its beneficial impact on circulation makes sure that the right volume of blood reaches the reproductive organs. By improving circulation, endometriosis and other pelvic congestion are reduced, and the pain associated with these conditions is lessened.

Side Effects

Although yarrow is a "natural" product, bear in mind that even natural compounds can have negative effects and drug interactions, and you should treat these items as you would prescription drugs. Although yarrow is typically thought to be safe for medical usage, some potential adverse effects include:

- Drowsiness
- Increased urination
- When used topically, it causes skin irritation (such as for wound healing)

However, taking yarrow supplements may pose significant dangers to some populations, for instance:

> ### Decreased blood clotting

A yarrow may, in theory, prevent blood coagulation. It is advisable that you cease taking yarrow at least two weeks before an operation. Tell the medical professionals about this potential risk if you req uire emergency surgery. Similar to that, those with known bleeding issues should refrain from using yarrow without first consulting a healthcare professional because it may raise the risk of bleeding.

> ### Allergies

You can also be allergic to yarrow if you're allergic to plants in the Asteraceae/Compositae family. Family members of the plant include:

- Chrysanthemums
- Daisies
- Marigolds
- Ragweed

Before using yarrow, see your doctor if you have plant allergies but are unsure whether they extend to this specific genus of plants.

> ➢ **Breastfeeding and pregnancy**

Neither nursing nor using yarrow while pregnant are advised. A woman's menstrual cycle may be influenced by yarrow when taken orally. This indicates that you could be at risk for miscarriage if you take it while pregnant. It is best to avoid using yarrow until after your kid has been weaned because we currently don't have sufficient knowledge of its potential risks during breastfeeding.

Tips For Use

For inflammatory diseases, 4.5 grams of yarrow herb per day is the normal dose. The dose, however, has not been validated by any recent clinical investigations.

How To Harvest Yarrow

The best time to cut yarrow is on a warm morning when the flowers are fully opened, the dew has evaporated, and the leaves are entirely green(vs starting to yellow and pass). The best day to accomplish this is one that is not raining. It will be possible for the plant to flower again in the same season if the top four inches of the plant, including the flower head, are removed just above a leaf node. The flower should blossom again, set seed, and grow additional flowers and plants. You can gather the herb's flower heads and leaves separately when foraging it in order to preserve it. Each of them is worth keeping for a different reason. Just before the multiple stems meet the long stem, remove the flower heads. Use pruners or kitchen shears for this. Simply hold the stem between your fingers and gently pull down to retain the leaves. The pile of leaves should form without difficulty.

6. Calendula

Due to its ease of cultivation and versatility as a medicinal plant, calendula (Calendula officinalis, Asteraceae), naturally finds its way into the gardens and hearts of all herb lovers. It has been used for ages to treat burns, rashes, and wounds both internally and topically. A traditional cure for boosting the immune system and improving the spirits uses sunny flowers. In addition, the flower heads' edible ray florets, which resemble yellow petals, are overflowing with anti-oxidant chemicals. Calendula's name stems from the Latin calendar and refers to its lengthy blooming period. In some regions, it is rumored to bloom almost every month of the year. Its historical use as the official medicinal species of its genus in apothecaries and pharmacopeias is referenced by the species name officinalis. Other names for calendula include marigold and pot marigold.

Health Benefits Of Calendula

Calendula is a true Jack of all trades. This plant, which can treat a variety of health conditions, can also spread throughout your entire house, from the yard, kitchen to the medicine cabinet. Let's look at some of its benefits:

➢ Heals Injuries

Calendula is applied topically to wounds to promote the growth of new tissue and keep them clean. It is freq uently used to aid in the course correction of wounds that are not healing properly and displaying symptoms of pain, redness, or inflammation. Sunburns and other mild burns can be effectively treated with the healing herb. Applying calendula lotion, ointment, or healing balm to wounds might help reduce swelling and speed up the healing process due to their antibacterial properties, particularly the antifungal compounds.

➢ Aids The Immune And Digestive Systems

Calendula's vulnerability can be utilized to combat any lingering infections caused by flu or a recently passed cold. It has been demonstrated that calendula increases the immune system's capacity to ward off infections. This is probably because calendula has antibacterial properties, which slow or eliminate an infection to stop it from spreading. It can combat that persistent cough or congestion you can't seem to get rid of, thanks to its antibacterial characteristics.

➢ Dry Skin Is Hydrated And Nourished

Numerous skin disorders that might result in dry, itchy, or irritated areas can be treated with calendula. It calms skin and experiences symptoms of eczema, dermatitis, and dandruff.

Calendula contributes to the maintenance of calmed, hydrated skin by encouraging the development of collagen, a necessary protein for radiant skin. Calendula has a powerful effect, but because of its softness, many people with sensitive skin can still benefit from its skincare properties.

➢ **Reduces The Rate Of Skin Aging**

Additionally, it has been discovered that calendula can help delay the appearance of wrinkles. Calendula's anti-inflammatory and antioxidant components have been found to significantly shield human skin cells from oxidative damage. Damage-causing atoms and antioxidants are out of eq uilibrium, causing oxidative stress. Oxidative stress is a major factor in both the aging process and the emergence of numerous diseases. Calendula makes it possible to maintain healthy, hydrated skin, making it an excellent ingredient in daily lotions or lip balm.

➢ **Getting Rid Of Scars**

When utilized to treat wounds, the significant benefit of calendula is its capacity to lessen scarring. The same q ualities of calendula that help with wound healing also aid with scarring. Calendula promotes a q uick and healthy healing process, is infection-free, and bolsters the growth of healthy new tissue while increasing blood flow to the wound. The plant softens and soothes the skin in situations of skin ulcers, like chicken pox and acne, avoiding inflammation and enhancing the immune response, which enables wounds to heal swiftly and thoroughly.

Side Effects

Some persons who are sensitive or allergic to pollen, such as ragweed or marigolds, also develop allergic reactions to calendula as a result of their primary allergy. Before you begin learning about the extraordinary advantages calendula has to offer, be on the lookout for it.

Tips For Use

Many skin care products, including soaps, creams, ointments, salves, and lotions with different amounts of calendula, contain extracts. To treat minor skin issues, apply preparations three to four times a day.

How To Harvest Calendula

Calendula blooms can be collected by picking or pruning the flower at the stem's intersection. Avoid gathering the heads that are beginning to dry and go to seed if you intend to utilise it as food or medicine.

For this, new flowers work best. Save your seed from the older ones instead. Take the entire head, of course! The green pedestal, not only the flower petals, has the greatest therapeutic potential. Some calendula cultivars have sturdy stems to make good-cut flowers as well, so you shouldn't worry if you don't want to dry or use the fresh blossoms.

7. Lavender

The Lamiaceae, or mint family, of blooming plants is referred to as lavender. Lavandula latifolia and Lavandula angustifolia are two of the most popular "lavenders." Other common names for Lavandula angustifolia include English lavender, French lavender, and real lavender. A spike lavender or spike is another name for Lavandula latifolia. The scented herb lavender (Lavandula angustifolia) is commonly utilized in the perfume industry. The essential oils made from lavender are widely used. The biological and health benefits of lavender oils are numerous. The Mediterranean region gave rise to the lavender plant.

The Varieties Of Lavender

Lavender is available in the following forms:

- Essential oil
- Extract
- Plant (flower, stem, and leaves)
- Tea

Health Benefits Of Lavender

The following are the benefits of lavender:

- ✓ **Promotes sleep: Lavender can raise** your body's melatonin levels, promoting greater sleep at night.

- ✓ **Reduces discomfort and swelling:** According to studies, lavender essential oil helps lessen headache discomfort.

- ✓ **Helps with depression, anxiety, and mood:** It is well known that lavender can soothe the nervous system, improve mood, and even lower blood pressure.

- ✓ **Reducing menstrual pain:** According to studies, pain levels decreased after two months for women who inhaled lavender for 30 minutes daily during the first three days of their periods.

- ✓ **Symptomatic relief for colic:** Infancy colic symptoms, such as the amount of time spent crying each week, were found to be significantly reduced by aromatherapy massage using lavender oil.

Side Effects

Oral supplements, such as lavender capsules, are also considered safe for short-term use. Depending on the sensitivity of your skin, lavender topical oil application can be done safely. The application of lavender oil can cause an allergic reaction in some people's skin. Before using lavender on your skin, always use a carrier oil and perform a patch test. To evaluate the safety of lavender in pregnant women or nursing, more research is req uired. Before initiating any treatment with lavender, consult your doctor if you have any of these disorders.

Tips For Use

In order to use lavender essential oil for aromatherapy, one to several drops (20 mg to 120 mg) should be diluted in a base or carrier oil, applied to hot water in a diffuser or humidifier, absorbed on a cotton pad, or poured into a jar for inhalation. Lavender herb can be soaked in a cup of boiling water for 1 to 2 tsp (5 to 10 mL) to make tea. For use in treating anxiety, a patented oral medication called Silexan is often dosed at 80 or 160 mg per day.

How To Harvest Lavender

Simply cut the stems just before the blooms open to harvest the lavender, and when you have enough for your req uirements, tie the stems together and hang them to dry in a protected area. The blossoms can be gently shook from the stalks and placed in a container once they have fully dried after a few weeks.

8. Chamomile

A member of the asteraceae family, chamomile (Matricaria Recutita) is a flowering plant. It was formerly found only throughout Europe and Western Asia.

The herb has a faint apple scent, which may help explain its name, chamomile, which is a Greek term for "Earth apple." German chamomile and Roman chamomile are two separate varieties of chamomile plants. The former is the most frequently used cultivar for therapeutic purposes and thought to be more powerful than the latter. Its other names are:

- Matricaria recutita
- Chamomilla recutita
- German chamomile
- Hungarian chamomile
- True chamomile

Health Benefits Of Chamomile

The following benefits of chamomile are listed even when it is consumed as tea:

> **Supportive of sleep**

The calming effects of chamomile tea are well recognized, and this may be because of the phytonutrients it contains, particularly a substance known as apigenin. According to studies, chamomile tea helps postpartum moms sleep better and with less depression.

➢ **Could reduce anxiety**

More research is req uired in this area, but evidence so far suggests that chamomile may be helpful for people with mild anxiety.

➢ **People with diabetes might benefit from it**

According to some theories, chamomile may assist persons with diabetes better regulate their blood sugar by lowering blood sugar levels and promoting better glycogen storage in the liver.

➢ **Digestive problems may be alleviated by it**

Inflammatory digestive conditions, like diverticulitis and oesophageal reflux, may be helped by chamomile, according to research, which may also aid to minimize smooth muscle spasms in the stomach. Additionally, it may provide protection from H. Pylori (also known as Helicobacter Pylori) bacteria, a common pathogen that can causes stomach ulcers.

➢ **Beneficial for cardiovascular health**

With their antioxidant qualities and potential benefits for lowering blood pressure and cholesterol, flavonoids, which are abundant in chamomile, are a class of chemicals.

Side Effects

People with allergies to ragweed and chrysanthemum may experience a reaction—sometimes a severe one—when using chamomile either ingested or applied topically because these plants are relatives of chamomile. Call your doctor if you experience vomiting, skin rashes, or allergic reactions (chest tightness, wheezing, hives, rash, or itching) after using chamomile, even though Roman chamomile is said to be more likely to cause responses.

Tips For Use

Take one to one and a half tablespoons of the flower and steep them in hot water for five minutes to make tea. This procedure can be repeated three to four times daily.

How To Harvest Chamomile

It's simple and relaxing to pick chamomile. Just below the blossom head, gently pinch the plant's stem. The flower head can then be removed by placing your fore and middle fingers underneath, between the flower and the other clenched fingers.

9. Mint

Mint is a leafy herb that, due to the chilly sensation it gives off in the mouth, is probably most known for its relationship with having fresh breath. Mint is a typical flavouring for chewing gum, breath mints, toothpaste, and mouthwash.

Mint is used to flavour dishes and beverages besides refreshing breath. Mint is renowned for giving lamb meals, mojito cocktails, and mint chocolate chip ice cream a bright flavor. The mint plant has many different types, and most of them belong to the genus Mentha. Mint plants proliferate rapidly, so gardeners typically cultivate them in containers. When planted straight into the ground, they can grow invasive and take over a garden. All continents other than Antarctica have native mint plants. There are many different types of mint, including water and wild mint, but peppermint and spearmint are probably the two most frequently used ones. The genus Monarda also includes certain plants known as "mint." The Lamiaceae family, which includes the genera Mentha and Monarda, is one unit. Horsemint, catmint, and stone mint are all Monarda mint varieties. All mint species can be utilised when fresh, dried, made into tea, or extracted into essential oils.

Health Benefits Of Mint

All around the world, mint leaves are frequently utilized. Its many uses range from making chutney to reviving mojitos. Given that it also has medicinal capabilities, in addition to adding an extra dash of flavor, freshness, and aroma, it can help you in a variety of ways. The benefits are:

➤ It treats every gastrointestinal ailment

Due to their anti-inflammatory properties, mint leaves can assist in lessening any stomach inflammation. Additionally, mint leaves can aid with dyspepsia.

➤ It strengthens your immunity

Phosphorus, calcium, and vitamins C, D, E, and A, which strengthen the immune system, are abundant in mint leaves. Additionally, it guards against cell damage, lowering your likelihood of developing any chronic illnesses.

➤ It gives you acne-free skin

It relaxes and calms your skin because of its anti-inflammatory and anti-bacterial characteristics, which might be helpful for treating acne. Salicylic acid, which is well known for treating pimples and acne, is abundant in mint leaves.

> **It beats nausea and morning sickness**

It can be an excellent treatment for morning sickness-related nausea because it is so effective at curing gastrointestinal problems. It combats motion sickness and activates the digestive enzymes. For expectant mothers who frequently have morning sickness, it might be a fantastic treatment.

> **Helps with asthma and allergies**

Rosmarinic acid, a potent antioxidant and anti-inflammatory, is found in mint leaves. Asthma and allergy sufferers benefit from this medication's blocking of allergy-inducing substances. **Side Effects**

Most people can safely consume mint leaves or apply the oil topically. Mint allergies are uncommon but can cause asthma attacks in those who are exposed to them. Fresh mint leaves or mint oil may infrequently result in adverse responses when consumed. The menthol in mint can cause heartburn, nausea, abdominal pain, and dry mouth when consumed in large doses. Peppermint should be avoided if you have gastroesophageal reflux illness. Those who have kidney stones should also avoid it. Certain drugs may interact with peppermint or have their effects diminished.

As some studies indicate, the herb may drop your blood sugar and pressure. It is not advisable for persons taking medication for diabetes or blood pressure disorders. The safety of consuming peppermint tea or utilizing peppermint oil during pregnancy or breast-feeding is not well understood. Therefore, before consuming the herbal beverage, pregnant women should see their doctors. It is not advisable to use peppermint oil on infants or young children because it could have a harmful impact on their breathing.

Tips For Use

IBS-related constipation and diarrhea have been treated with enteric-coated capsules containing up to 1,200 mg of peppermint oil per day (180 to 400 mg three times per day).

How To Harvest Mint

Mint plants are easy to harvest; there is no secret. If you only need a few leaves, you can pick them off the plant one at a time or prune it with shears before removing the leaves from the stems.

10. Passionflower

A herbal medicine called passionflower (passiflora incarnata) has traditionally been used to treat hysteria, sleeplessness, anxiety, and seizures. The passionflower is a perennial climbing vine that was once only grown in the Southeast of North America. The plant's stems, leaves, and flowers are used to make a herbal supplement. Passionflower can be purchased as tinctures, infusions, teas, liq uid extracts, and teas for use in complementary medicine.

Health Benefits Of Passionflower

There are both wild and domesticated forms of the stunning flower known as the passionflower. It is a key plant used to treat pain, nerve problems, and sleeplessness since it is a potent nervine, sedative, and analgesic. These benefits are explained below:

> **Anxiety/Depression**

The herb passionflower may be the most helpful if depression and menopause are associated. The alkaloids "chrysin" and "benzoflavone" found in this herb have been found to boost GABA (gamma amino-butyric acid) in the brain, in addition to easing symptoms, like hot flashes and night sweats, which are already dismal enough. The brain uses GABA, one of the inhibitory neurotransmitters, to maintain equilibrium and prevent overexcitation. It also aids in reducing the activity of brain cells that cause depression.

➤ Insomnia

Passionflower is a somewhat sedative and anti-anxiety plant that can even be used to get kids to sleep through the night. In one study, participants who had problems sleeping were encouraged to consume a cup of passionflower tea before bed for a specified period. All the volunteers reported seeing noticeable improvements in their sleep. The increased GABA that passionflower might cause in the brain can help lessen the anxiety that is frequently linked to sleeplessness. As a muscle relaxant, passionflower is also believed to help people fall asleep more easily by releasing tension.

➤ Antioxidant/Anti-inflammatory

Due to the presence of the antioxidant components vitexin, isovitexin, kaempferol, quercetin, rutin, apigenin, and luteolin glycosides, passionflower has a strong antioxidant effect. Indole alkaloids, fatty acids, gum, maltol, phytosterols, sugars, and minute amounts of volatile oils are also present. One substance, in particular, quercetin, has received a great deal of attention. It has been discovered to be incredibly powerful at removing harmful free radical molecules from the body and inhibiting a number of enzymes that contribute to inflammation. These substances also calm the neurological system, which helps reduce nerve-related pain, such as backache.

> ➤ **Lowers Blood Pressure**

According to studies, taking a passionflower extract helps lower blood pressure (hypertension).

It was discovered that drinking one cup of passionflower tea daily can help patients with mild hypertension control their blood pressure levels. It is crucial to remember that folks on blood pressure medication shouldn't use this herb because it can dangerously drop blood pressure.

Side Effects

When used as a food flavouring, passionflower is probably safe for the majority of individuals. When consumed as tea every night for seven nights or as medicine for up to eight weeks, it might be safe. When used orally in significant doses, such as 3.5 grammes of a specific extract over two days, it may be dangerous. Drowsiness, vertigo, and disorientation are some of the negative effects of passionflower. The safety of applying passionflower to the skin is not adequately understood. **Tips For Use**

The following dose ranges are typical for adults:

- ✓ 0.75 to 6 g/day of the plant's dried aerial portions, prepared as an infusion.
- ✓ A liq uid extract of a ratio of 1:1, 1.5–3 ml/day.
- ✓ 3 to 6 mL of a 1:2 liq uid extract daily, or an equal amount in a pill or tablet.
- ✓ 1.5-8 mL of a 1:8 tincture every day.

How To Harvest Passionflower

Harvesting should take place in the morning after the dew has evaporated. Look for wide-open passionflowers. Use shears to cut off the flower stem at the vine as you remove individual blossoms from the vine. Cut the passionflower's stem at the base from the back.

11. Rose

Rose is a herb that develops into a little shrub. A rose is either a floral plant of the genus Rosa, family Rosaceae, or a woody perennial plant. This plant is widely grown around the world for both beauty and therapeutic purposes. This plant can reach a height of 7 meters and has spikes that grow to a height of 1.5 to 2 meters. Its size can vary from compact to miniature. Typically, it is grown for its fragrant blossoms, which are sold commercially. The leaflets on this plant's alternately growing leaves are oval in shape and have sharp teeth. These plant's tasty, fleshy fruits, known as rose hips when ripe, are luscious and plentiful.

The many varieties of garden roses are a result of the ease with which species from many parts of the world can hybridize.

Health Benefits Of Roses

These are the benefits of roses:

- Hormone balance (including amenorrhea)
- Decrease eye and skin inflammation
- Relieve coughs and sore throats
- Encourage sound, quiet sleep
- Cool the digestive system
- Calm tense, furious, and depressed feelings
- May slow down skin aging and decrease wrinkles
- Their analgesic actions could perhaps lessen pain
- Strong antibacterial and sanitizing q ualities
- Bring down blood sugar levels

- The ability to protect the brain
- Possess antioxidant properties

A rose can be found in a variety of items that can be applied externally or internally, including:

- Rose essential oil (great for aromatherapy and for use in beauty products)
- Rose water (delicious in food and beverage recipes as well as to soothe the skin)
- Rose hydrosol (a cooling and hydrating skin toner)
- Rosebud jam (a sweet uplifting treat)
- Rose tea (wonderful benefits for soothing the mind, heart, and throat)
- Rose powder (useful in herbal formulas, skin products, and culinary recipes)

The rose's volatile oil (as well as more than 100 other currently known constituents) has a variety of medicinal benefits, including antidepressant, highly antioxidant, antispasmodic, aphrodisiac, astringent, antibacterial, antiviral, antiseptic, strongly anti-inflammatory, blood tonic, cleansing, cooling, digestive stimulant, expectorant, bile production stimulant, kidney tonic, and menstrual regulator. Rose makes a nice addition to tea or gargle for a sore throat because of its astringent properties.

Its antibacterial and antiviral properties can aid in the treatment of intestinal infections. Additionally, it provides excellent immune system support, making it helpful in instances of cold and flu. Rose tea or a poultice made of leaves and petals can be used as a calming and energizing facial. Rose water has been used for the skin for a long time. Make sure to steep some rose petals in vinegar because it helps soothe sunburn, makes a great hair rinse, and makes an unusual addition to sauces or dressings. Rashes and dry, itchy skin can benefit greatly from rose petal tea or a salve produced by steeping petals in oil. The rose, more than anything else, opens the heart to hope. It eases anxiety and acts as a nerve tonic that cools and calms.

The rose will soothe the tension and help the organs that must eliminate the toxins these emotions hurl into the circulation for persons who are dealing with self-doubt, worry, or perimenopause. Do you realize that neither roses nor rosehips are flowers? In actuality, rosehips are the rose plant's seed pods. This seed pod resembles a fruit, even a crabapple. You don't see rosehips very often because rose bushes are freq uently clipped. Rosehips have almost all of the therapeutic benefits of the petals and are also rich in bioflavonoids. Rosehip seed oil, a fixed oil (not an essential oil), is well known for reducing or eliminating scar tissue. It also regenerates skin, delays the onset of wrinkles, calms psoriasis and dermatitis, treats burns, and aids in the restoration of the tone and color of injured skin.

Side Effects

Rosehips freq uently cause these side effects:

- Renal stones
- Nausea

- Vomiting

- Diarrhea

- Constipation

- Heartburn

- Stomach pain

- Fatigue

- Headache

- Difficult sleeping

- An allergic response (from inhaling rosehip dust)

Tips For Use

Adults have most frequently taken rosehip in oral doses of up to 5 grams per day for up to 12 weeks. Find out from a healthcare professional what dosage might be appropriate for your condition.

How To Harvest Roses

Trim the stem at an angle, remove the bottom leaves, and put it in a vase with fresh water. To promote new bloom, get rid of wilted flowers. To develop thicker, stronger stems, deadhead single-flower roses back to the first 5-leaf leaf. Only eliminate individual flowers when they wither from a cluster.

12. Aloe Vera

For thousands of years, people have utilized the medicinal plant aloe vera (Aloe barbadensis) to treat a variety of illnesses. Aloe vera can be used directly from the plant or purchased in gel form, and it is typically safe to do so. It is a pea-green perennial shrubby or arborescent plant that is xerophytic and a member of the Liliaceae family. The transparent gel contained in aloe vera leaves is what's used in aloe vera lotions, gels, and ointments. Different skin diseases can be treated topically with these products. Aloe vera is available for purchase as a liq uid or capsule to be taken internally to support health and wellbeing.

Health Benefits Of Aloe Vera

The following are among the many health benefits of aloe vera:

➢ Higher Rate Of Wound Healing

The most typical application of aloe vera is as a topical agent, which involves rubbing it on the skin. It has long been used to treat burns and wounds. In fact, it's a medicine that works well to speed up recovery from burns. How can aloe vera promote q uicker healing of wounds? A polymer called glucomannan and growth hormone called gibberellin are both found in aloe vera.

The fibroblast's growth factor receptors are the means via which these interact. The proliferation of the fibroblasts is conseq uently induced, enhancing collagen synthesis. As a result, the procedure speeds up wound healing.

➢ Defending The Skin

Aloe vera has been proved to protect the skin after numerous tests. It shields the skin from radiation's negative skin-damaging effects and free radical damage. Aloe vera gel creates metallothionein, a powerful antioxidant protein, and protects against hydroxyl radicals when applied to the skin, albeit the precise method is unknown.

➢ Treat Insect Bites

Aloe vera has been used to calm insect bites because it contains substances that stop inflammation. Aloe vera also functions as an antipruritic when applied to the skin, which lessens or stops itching.

➢ Anti-Inflammatory

Aloe vera is an efficient anti-inflammatory. It lessens arachidonic acid's ability to produce prostaglandin E2 by inhibiting the cyclooxygenase pathway. Aloe vera also functions as an antioxidant that combats free radicals, a common source of oxidative damage and inflammation.

➢ Supports Digestion

Digestion support is one of aloe vera's most well-known health advantages. Aloe vera juice consumption enhances digestion and alleviates gastroesophageal reflux disease, hyperacidity, and ulcers (GERD).

Side Effects

Aloe vera may carry some hazards in addition to its many health benefits. Among these include:

➢ Skin allergies

Aloe vera's components may cause hypersensitivity in certain persons. Aloe vera gel usage over a long time can also result in skin allergies, like hives and irritation.

➢ Diarrhea

Some individuals who have used aloe vera as a laxative or for digestion have reported experiencing diarrhea and upset stomach. Dehydration and an electrolyte imbalance from untreated diarrhea can be hazardous.

➢ Reduced Blood Sugar

Aloe vera can help lower blood sugar levels. To avoid dangerously low blood sugar levels, diabetic persons who take medications to decrease their blood glucose should exercise caution if they also use aloe vera.

Tips For Use

For burns and other skin disorders, apply to the skin many times each day. Take 10 to 20 ml (about one tablespoon) twice daily for diabetes and 25 to 30 ml (about two teaspoons) twice daily for colitis. You may also adhere to the manufacturer's instructions.

How To Harvest Aloe Vera

Aloe vera plants can be easily harvested for their juice and gel. A mature plant that is at least a few years old will be necessary. As a result, the active compounds are concentrated more. Additionally, you should give the same plant a few weeks before cutting any leaves. If you intend to harvest aloe vera freq uently, you might wish to keep a few plants in rotation. To get the gel and juice from your aloe plant:

- Choose thick leaves from the plant's outer portions and remove 3–4 at a time.

- Make sure the leaves are sound and unharmed by mold.

- Trim them just above the stem. The majority of the healthy nutrients can be located at the root of the plant.

- Beware of the roots.

- Dry and wash the leaves.

- Cut off the sharp edges with a knife.

- Separate the leaf's internal gel from the exterior using a knife or your fingertips. The component of the aloe vera you'll use is the inner gel.

- Permit the leaf's golden sap to drain. The aloe vera latex is shown here. This can be contained if you intend to utilise latex. You can get rid of the latex if you don't plan to use it.

- Slice or cut the aloe gel into cubes.

After extracting the aloe from the leaf's outer layer, you can put the aloe into a blender and then drain the mixture to get smooth aloe gel.

13. Bilberry

The European berry known as the bilberry has a dark blue skin. The name whortleberry, huckleberry, or blaeberry have all been used. Bilberries (Vaccinium myrtillus) first resemble blueberries in appearance. The two berries are related and have comparable nutritional properties, but they also differ in a few ways. When in season, the flesh of the two berries has one of the most obvious variations between them: a different hue. In contrast to bilberries, which have a red or purple appearance, blueberries have a greenish color inside their dark blue skins. Bilberries and blueberries have a more acidic flavor than one another in addition to their variances in hue. Even though these berries are tiny, they have a wide range of incredible health benefits.

Health Benefits Of Bilberry

The following are the benefits:

➢ **Reduced Inflammation**

Antioxidants included in bilberries may help your body experience less inflammation, which reduces your risk of developing inflammatory illnesses, like cancer, diabetes, and heart disease.

➤ Decreased Danger Of Alzheimer's Disease

Bilberries contain phenolic acids, which, according to studies, may help lower your risk of getting Alzheimer's disease.

➤ Digestive Wellness

Digestion problems can be helped by bilberry. Your digestive system's inflammation can be reduced by the antioxidants, tannins, and pectin found in berries. Diarrhea, motion sickness, and indigestion are reduced by decreasing this inflammation.

➤ Reduced Risk Of Diabetes

Blood sugar levels can be lowered in diabetics by bilberries and bilberry extract. In those who have metabolic syndrome, the berries may also help boost insulin secretion.

➤ Lower Risk Of Developing Heart Disease

Bilberries provide vitamin K, which can aid in preventing blood clots that might result in heart attack or stroke. In addition to lowering blood pressure and cholesterol, bilberries' anthocyanins may also do so. Keeping your blood pressure and cholesterol under control will lower your risk of developing atherosclerosis and other heart-related issues.

➢ Reduction Of Cancer

Anthocyanins, vitamin C, and other antioxidants found in bilberries aid in the body's defense against free radicals. Bilberries may lessen your risk of acq uiring some types of cancer by defending against free radicals and cell damage.

Side Effects

There are extra risks to consider before consuming bilberry.

✓ Overdosing

The risk of overdosing may be increased by combining several bilberry products. Unless otherwise instructed, limit yourself to using only one type of bilberry at a time. There are several bilberry formulations, such as tinctures, extracts, teas, and supplements. Nevertheless, there are no cases of overdoses connected to bilberry.

✓ Responses To Allergies

Bilberry allergies are uncommon, although they can happen with any plant. You might want to err on the side of caution and steer clear of bilberry if you have a plant allergy to the Ericaceae family or anthocyanosides. The symptoms of an allergic reaction include the following:

- Anxiety
- Confusion
- Rash

- Hives

- Diarrhea

- Nausea

- Vomiting

- Throat constriction

- Having trouble breathing

- Inflammation of the skin

- Lips, tongue, or face swelling

Seek emergency medical assistance if any of these symptoms apply to you or someone you know.

Tips For Use

It can be used for the following:

- ✓ **Vibrant berries:** One cup of fresh fruit per day. If bilberries are not available, American blueberries may be substituted.

- ✓ **Tea:** Two cups of water and one spoonful of dried berries should simmer for twenty minutes. Strain. For diarrhea, consume 1/2 cup every 3 to 4 hours.

- ✓ **Extracts:** The dosage range for an extract standardized to include 25% anthocyanosides is typically 360 to 600 mg per day (also written as anthocyanins).

How to Harvest

Berries are twig-borne singly rather than in clusters. Pick them when they are approximately 1 cm in diameter, all the same hue (a darker shade of purple than the blueberry), and in the late summer. Pick a few berries each day as they ripen on the bush.

14. Black Cohosh

Black cohosh is a blooming perennial plant with fragrant white blossoms on a stalk that may grow up to five feet tall and is scientifically known as Actaea racemosa or cimicifuga racemosa. It is a member of the buttercup family and found in eastern North America's forests. There are additional names for black cohosh, including:

- Black bugbane.
- Black snakeroot.
- Fairy candle.
- Macrotys.
- Rattleweed.
- Rheumatism weed.

Health Benefits Of Black Cohosh

These are the benefits:

> ➢ **The menopause's symptoms**

Menopause symptoms, including hot flashes, appear to be lessened by taking a special black cohosh supplement called Remifemin, made by Phytopharmica/Enzymatic Therapy. However, not all products containing black cohosh may offer these advantages. Several alternative uses of black cohosh are being considered, but there isn't enough solid evidence to indicate if they would be beneficial. Black cohosh may provide a number of advantages, with most of them being connected to women's health or hormonal balance. However, other than menopause symptoms, there isn't much data to back up its usage for any of these issues.

Side Effects

When used properly, black cohosh may be safe for up to a year. It may result in moderate side effects, such as nausea, headaches, rashes, and a heavy feeling. Additionally, some people worry that black cohosh may harm their livers in rare cases. Black cohosh users should keep an eye out for signs of liver damage, such as lethargy and dark urine.

Tips For Use

It can be used for the following:

> ✓ **Pediatric**

Black cohosh is not currently recommended for children, and there are no documented research findings on its use in youngsters.

✓ **Adults**

Black cohosh is taken daily in doses ranging from 20 to 80 mg. The dosage of 27-deoxyactein should be standardized at 1 mg per pill. For black cohosh tincture, that is 2 to 4 ml, diluted in water or tea once to three times a day. The daily dose is usually given in two capsules or tablets. Although they have been used historically, teas might not be as efficient as the black cohosh standardized extract in reducing menopausal symptoms.

Pour 20 g of the dried root into 34 oz of water to make a black cohosh beverage. Bring to a boil, then reduce the liq uid by one-third by simmering for 20 to 30 minutes. Strain, cover, and keep chilled or in a dry, cool place. Up to 48 hours are possible with the drink. Consume one cup three times a day.

How To Harvest Black Cohosh

Before the plant dies back in fall, the majority of black cohosh is picked. The weight and bioactive components of the roots are at their highest point at this time. The entire root is collected, including the fibrous roots and rhizome. Typically, digging is done by hand with a spading fork. Remove any remaining soil by shaking the extracted roots, and then carefully sort out any roots that aren't black cohosh. It is necessary to get rid of all soil, sand, rocks, and other foreign objects.

Avoid letting the newly collected roots dry up by shielding them from the sun and heat. If the roots are going to be used as planting stock, they should either be planted right away or combined with moist sphagnum moss and kept in a cooler at around 40°F in mesh bags, burlap bags, or cardboard boxes. To avoid mold and mildew, stir the roots constantly and check freq uently to make sure they don't dry out. Wash the roots well with a pressure water hose or a root washer if they will be sold for use in creating a herbal product. A typical root washer comprises a revolving drum with water nozzles placed to fully clean the roots as they tumble.

15. Cayenne

The cayenne pepper (Capsicum annum) is probably known to those who enjoy spice. A Solanaceae plant, the long, thin, bright red Capsicum annum belongs to this family. It shares a kinship with other types of capsicum, such as the infamously hot ghost peppers, sweet bell peppers, jalapenos, poblanos, and serranos. The cayenne pepper still has a lot of heat, although not q uite as intense as the ghost pepper. According to legend, the cayenne pepper came from Cayenne, French Guiana. It is normally dried and ground into a fine powder. It is also used fresh in several dishes. It isgrown all over the world, including in Mexico, East Africa, India, and some regions of the United States. In addition to being delicious, it gives your food a little heat and has amazing health benefits.

Health Benefits Of Cayenne

Numerous health benefits can be derived from cayenne peppers. These comprise:

> **Reduced pain**

Like other hot peppers, cayenne peppers contain capsaicin, the substance that gives them their "heat." By reducing the amount of substance P, a neuropeptide that signals pain to the brain when applied topically, capsaicin can aid in pain relief.

➤ Therapy for psoriasis

Itchy, scaly, and red areas of skin are a symptom of the autoimmune disease psoriasis. Topical capsaicin creams can assist to lessen irritation and enhance the appearance of the skin, despite the fact that there is presently no treatment.

➤ Improved metabolism

Capsaicin causes your body to produce more heat, which somewhat speeds up your metabolism and increases the amount of calories you burn. You may eat less throughout the day as a result of its modest effectiveness in lowering hunger.

➤ Digestive wellness

The stomach's nerves that transmit signals for damage prevention are stimulated by capsaicin. In addition to sending digestive enzymes to the stomach to aid in digestion, the pepper may also give the stomach greater defense against infections.

➤ Lowering blood pressure

According to research conducted with animals, cayenne (capsaicin) may help lower high blood pressure, which, in turn, reduces the risk of developing heart disease.

> **Lowering the risk for cancer**

According to certain research, capsaicin can decrease the growth of cancer cells. Some cancers, such as prostate, skin, and pancreatic, may even be susceptible to its ability to eradicate cancer cells.

Side Effects

Some people can experience allergic reactions to several foods. However, cayenne pepper allergy is uncommon. But anyone who consumes cayenne pepper and has hives, swelling, or trouble breathing should seek emergency medical treatment. Anaphylaxis, a severe reaction that can be fatal, can develop from an allergic reaction. A doctor should be consulted before taking capsaicin for medical purposes.

Tips For Use

Cayenne pepper is more freq uently seen in your local grocery shop among other spices as a ground spice. In the produce area of some stores, you can find fresh peppers. Look for peppers that are firm, shiny, and brilliant when purchasing them fresh. Avoid items that have dark blotches, wrinkles, or are sq uishy. Fresh cayennes can be kept in your refrigerator's vegetable drawer by placing them in a paper bag or wrapping them in paper towels. Avoid using plastic bags since they can retain moisture and hasten the deterioration of your peppers. When you're ready to utilise them, wash them only then. There are several uses for cayenne pepper, both fresh and ground:

- To a soup or stew, sprinkle some cayenne pepper on top.

- It can be topped with scrambled eggs, q uiches, or egg salad.

- Add it to the hummus.

- When making hot chocolate, a little of cayenne pepper should be added.

- Make your lemonade and add this for a great boost.

- Sautéed vegetables can be spiced up with fresh or ground cayenne.

- Include fresh peppers in your preferred cornbread recipe.

- Cooked bitter greens, like collards or kale, should be combined with fresh peppers and lemon juice.

How To Harvest Cayenne Pepper

Cayenne peppers are often ready for harvesting between 70 and 100 days after planting. Red, 4 to 6 inches long (depending on the type), with waxy skin, and firm to the touch are the typical characteristics of ripe peppers. When the peppers reach this stage, harvest them. Soft, overripe specimens are not edible. However, the peppers won't taste as strong or matured if you consume them when they are still green. Although peppers can be harvested by pulling them from the stem, using pruners is advised to avoid injuring the entire stem. Just a little stem should be left on each pepper. Peppers can be stored for up to a year, and they can be kept for about a week in the refrigerator. Alternately, you might dry them and then powder them for seasoning.

16. Chaste Tree Berry

A plant called vitex (Vitex agnus-castus) is utilized in herbal medicine. It's also known as chaste tree or chaste berry and frequently used to treat women's health issues. The fruit and/or seed from the plant that produces vitex are often extracted and used in supplements. It is unknown how exactly vitex works; however, it may indirectly affect a number of hormones, including prolactin, progesterone, and estrogen. As an illustration, it is believed that vitex inhibits prolactin secretion via stimulating dopamine receptors. The pituitary gland produces the hormone prolactin, which aids in promoting milk production and breast development.

Health Benefits Of Chaste Tree

Premenstrual syndrome (PMS), acne, fibrocystic breast disease, infertility in women, heavy menstrual bleeding, menopausal symptoms, insufficient production of breast milk, benign prostatic hyperplasia in men (BPH), migraine headaches, and joint disorders are just a few of the conditions for which chaste tree berry (Vitex agnus-castus) has a long history of use in herbal medicine. Chaste tree berries, also known as vitex or chaste berries, may have an impact on hormone levels by promoting the release of luteinizing hormone, which then raises progesterone levels (a hormone known to play a key role in regulating the menstrual cycle). It's also believed to impact prolactin, which is involved in promoting breast growth and milk production. In other words, the benefits are:

> **Utilizing Chaste Tree Berry For Hormone And PMS Issues**

Chaste tree berries are most freq uently used to treat PMS. It's safe to say that in modern Western herbal medicine, this berry is the most widely used PMS treatment. Chaste tree berries are very popular among German health practitioners for treating a variety of female hormonal problems. Chaste tree berries appeared to be effective in the treatment of premenstrual syndrome, according to a recent analysis of 12 studies looking at the berries' effects on women's health. Another study that involved 60 women between the ages of 18 and 44 found that chaste tree berries lessened premenstrual bloating, irritability, headaches, and skin problems. Chaste tree berries are freq uently used in Europe to treat breast discomfort (mastodynia). Menopause symptoms can be relieved by chaste tree berries.

> **Boosting Fertility With Chaste Tree Berry**

It's possible that this powerful berry will increase fertility. According to studies, 26% of participants had gotten pregnant three months after taking a supplement comprising chaste tree berry, green tea, L-arginine, vitamins (including folate), and minerals (compared to 10 percent of those who took the placebo). Treatment with chaste tree berries may also be beneficial for PCOS (polycystic ovary syndrome).

Side Effects

When eaten properly, the fruit of vitex agnus-castus is probably safe for the majority of individuals. Uncommon adverse reactions can include weight gain, bloating, nausea, headaches, itching, rash, and acne. When they begin using vitex agnus-castus, some women experience a change in their menstrual flow. When used properly on the skin, vitex agnus-castus seed extract is likely to be safe.

Tips For Use

The following are tips on how you can use chaste tree berry:

- ✓ **Tea:** Steep 1 cup of boiling water with 1/2 teaspoon of dried chaste tree fruit for 5 to 7 minutes. Take one cup in the morning. The tea has an unpleasant flavor and is a little peppery.
- ✓ **Capsules:** Dried chaste tree fruit capsules containing 250–500 mg should be taken once daily.
- ✓ **Tincture:** Take 2 to 3 cc of tincture every morning.
- ✓ **Extract:** One daily dose of 20–40 mg of chaste tree extract.

How To Harvest Chaste Tree Berry (Vitex agnus-castus)

Fruits should be picked while they are green to light purple rather than waiting until they have turned brown. Harvesting is simple; just slide the entire spike through your hand and remove the berries.

17. Chocolate

Theobroma cacao tree seeds, from which cacao is manufactured, are used to make chocolate. "Food of the gods" is how the Greek word theobroma is translated. Tropical rainforests in South and Central America support this kind of tree. It has a uniq ue combination of elements, including humidity and shade, that it req uires to develop. Nobody knows why the cocoa tree is so prevalent in some wilderness; it may be that it outcompetes other trees or these wild populations are a result of extensive plantations that were developed hundreds of years ago. As a result of its distinctive, rich, and sweet flavor, chocolate has since become a widely consumed food item. How does consuming chocolate, nevertheless, affect our health? That takes us to the benefits.

Health Benefits Of Chocolate

The benefits are:

> **Improvements In Heart Health**

The antioxidants in dark chocolate have been demonstrated to lower blood pressure, lessen the risk of clotting, and enhance blood flow to the heart, consequently reducing the risks of stroke, coronary heart disease, and heart disease-related death.

> **The Immune System Is In Balance**

Flavonols guard against the immune system overreacting and lessen oxidative stress, which is an imbalance brought on by cells fighting off free radicals and a common root cause of many diseases.

> **Prevents Diabetes**

Epicatechin helps the body utilise insulin more effectively, which may help prevent or treat diabetes. It also strengthens and protects cells.

> **Enhances Brain Activity**

Dark chocolate flavonols improve memory, reaction time, and visual-spatial awareness, among other aspects of brain function. The fact that flavonols improve blood flow to the brain may be one explanation for this; however, the study is still underway.

➤ Increases Physical Performance

Dark chocolate's epicatechin improves the blood's nitric oxide synthesis, promoting circulation and lowering the amount of oxygen an athlete needs while performing moderately demanding exercise. As a result, the athlete can continue working out at a high intensity for longer.

➤ Lessens Tension

Researchers confirmed that there were lower levels of the stress hormone cortisol after eating dark chocolate, and people who consumed it claimed to feel less anxious. Given that stress is a risk factor for cardiovascular disease, this may be connected to the positive benefits of dark chocolate on heart health.

If it isn't currently a part of your life, you should think about incorporating dark chocolate due to its health-promoting minerals and chemicals (it is important to note that dark chocolate contains caffeine, which some people may be sensitive to).

Side Effects

Consuming cocoa is probably safe for the majority of people when taken orally. But remember that chocolate also includes molecules connected to caffeine. The side effects of caffeine, such as anxiousness, increased urination, insomnia, and a rapid heartbeat, may be brought on by excessive consumption. Both allergic skin responses and migraines may be brought on by cocoa. Additionally, it may result in gas, constipation, nausea, and stomach discomfort. For the majority of people, applying cocoa butter to the skin is probably harmless. Some people may get a rash as a result.

Tips For Use

To get the most polyphenols and health advantages from this delightful treat, choose dark chocolate that has at least 70% cacao.

How To Harvest Cocoa

On the trunk and branches of the cocoa tree, pods carrying cocoa beans sprout. The process of harvesting entails taking ripe pods off the trees and opening them to remove the wet beans. By using a clean cut and sharp blade, one can manually harvest the pods by slicing through the stem. A tool similar to a pruning hook with a handle on the end of a long pole can be used for pods that are high on the tree. The upper and lower blades of the instrument allow the stalk to be cleanly chopped without harming the branch bearing it by pushing or pulling depending on where the fruit is located. Within a week to ten days following harvest, the pods are opened to extract the beans. The harvested pods are often gathered and divided on or near the plantation's edge. Before splitting, the pods may occasionally be moved to a fragmentary. The husks can be scattered around the fields to replenish the soil's nutrients if the pods are cracked open in the planting zones.The most effective method of opening the pods is to use a wooden club, which, when struck in the center of the pod, splits it into half, making it simple to extract the wet beans by hand. To split the pod, people frequently use a machete, albeit doing so can harm the beans.

Although some equipment has been created for opening the pod, smallholders often do it by hand. The beans go through a fermenting and drying process after being removed from the pod before being packed for distribution.

18. Cinnamon

Spice cinnamon (Cinnamomum Verum) is commonly used in lattes and as a garnish on toast. But for thousands of years, extracts from the cinnamon tree's bark, leaves, blossoms, fruits, and roots have also been utilized in traditional medicines around the world. It is added to many foods and used in baking and cooking.

Health Benefits Of Cinnamon

Cinnamaldehyde is one of the most significant active components in cinnamon. It is utilized in scents and flavorings. It might be the cause of some of cinnamon's potential health advantages. According to certain studies, cinnamon may benefit diabetics. In diabetics, it may also decrease cholesterol. Numerous studies lack information about the sort of cinnamon they used or have other issues that cast doubt on the accuracy of their conclusions. According to one analysis, cinnamon may aid in reducing obesity and weight gain. Irritable bowel syndrome and other stomach and intestinal issues are occasionally treated with it. But its effectiveness is unclear. Cinnamon has been proposed to be beneficial for:

- Heart condition
- Alzheimer's condition
- Cancer
- HIV
- Infection
- Dental decay
- Allergies

Although there are currently insufficient studies to support cinnamon's efficacy in treating human ailments, it has antioxidant, antibacterial, and anti-inflammatory qualities.

Side Effects

The side effects of cinnamon are:

> **Allergies and irritability**

Cinnamon often has no negative side effects. But its freq uent use could itch your lips and tongue, leading to ulcers. Some people react negatively to cinnamon. If you apply it to your skin, it could irritate and produce redness.

> **Toxicity**

Cassia cinnamon may be harmful if consumed in large quantities, especially if you have liver issues. Although the amount you would consume is so small that it probably won't be an issue, the component coumarin, found in some cinnamon products, might cause liver problems. Children, pregnant women, and nursing mothers should not use cinnamon for treatment due to the lack of safety data.

> **Decreased blood sugar**

If you have diabetes and take cinnamon supplements, you may need to modify your therapy. Cinnamon may alter your blood sugar levels.

> **Interactions**

Before beginning to use supplements containing cinnamon, discuss with your doctor whether you routinely take any medications. They might alter how treatments for diabetes, blood thinning, the heart, and other conditions operate.

Tips For Use

Powdered cinnamon spice is an alternative for diabetics, but it must be used daily at a dose of about one teaspoon to have a good impact on blood sugar levels. Cassia cinnamon is not always the typical spice bought in supermarkets.

Studies on type 1 and 2 diabetics employed 1 to 6 grams of cinnamon per day, administered in divided doses. Cinnamon capsules vary in dosage and recommended use.

How To Harvest Cinnamon

To harvest cinnamon, you must cut down a piece of the cinnamon tree and strip off the topmost layer of the bark. Scrape the cinnamon layer off in sheets with a paint scraper, and then allow the cinnamon to cure in a warm area. Cinnamon can be used either in its curled-up state or as powder.

19. Cranberry

The fruits called cranberries (Vaccinium macrocarpon) are grown in the Northeastern and North Central regions of the United States.

Bearberries and American cranberries are other names for cranberries. They are harvested in the US and Canada between the months of September and October. Cranberries are harvested using either a wet or dry harvest method. In the case of a wet harvest, the cranberry fields are submerged, and the floating fruits are harvested; in the case of a dry harvest, no water is used. While dry harvest fruit is cleaned and packaged as fresh fruit, wet harvest fruit is utilized to make processed cranberry juice and sauce.

Health Benefits Of Cranberries

Cranberries are widely known for their antimicrobial properties. These are its benefits:

> **Preventing urinary tract infections**

Traditional remedies for genitourinary infections have used cranberry.

➤ Treating gastric ulcers

Cranberry has demonstrated efficacy in the treatment of sores brought on by Helicobacter pylori because of its antibacterial qualities.

Cranberries are regarded to be beneficial in avoiding the development of dental plaq ue due to their capacity to suppress oral microorganisms. Additionally, preliminary studies have suggested novel benefits for cranberries, such as elevating "good" cholesterol levels and inhibiting some viruses.

Side Effects

Very few negative effects of cranberries are recognized. Overindulgence, however, might result in diarrhea and digestive problems.

Tips For Use

The simple and delicious method of preventing urinary tract infections is cranberry juice. Ten ounces of Ocean Spray cranberry juice were consumed daily in one well-designed trial. When compared to juice, cranberry extract in tablet form has been demonstrated to be eq ually effective, tolerable, affordable, and calorie-efficient. Taken twice daily, the recommended amount of concentrated juice extract is 300 to 500 mg.

How To Harvest Cranberries

Most industrial growers prefer wet harvesting since it yields the greatest amount of berries. About 99% of the crop is harvested wet, compared to only about 1/3 harvested dry. It is necessary to heat the wet gathered berries before making juice or sauce. So, how exactly does wet harvesting operate? Cranberries float because they have air spaces inside, making it easier to remove the fruit from the plant in flooded bogs. The berries from the vines are stirred up by water reels or "egg-beaters," which causes the fruit to float on the water surface. The berries are then gathered by plastic or wooden "booms." They are then transferred from the conveyor or pump to a vehicle and driven away for cleaning and processing. This method is used to gather more than 90% of all commercial cranberries. The dry technique of picking cranberries produces less fruit, but it is of the greatest caliber. Cranberries that have been collected in the dry state are sold intact. Cranberries are picked by mechanical pickers, which resemble enormous lawnmowers, using their metal teeth to pull them from the vine and put them into burlap sacks. The gathered berries are then flown to trucks using helicopters. A bounce board separator is used to separate the fresh berries from those that have passed their prime.

Freshest, firmest berries bounce back better than deteriorated or old fruit. About 400 to 600 farm laborers were req uired to manually select the berries before the invention of machinery to assist in the process. So, either flood them (which might not be realistic) or dry-pick them if you're growing and picking your cranberries. Make sure the weather is dry before doing this. The suiable berries for picking should have a firm texture and a red to dark crimson color. To check that your ripe cranberries are nice and springy after harvesting, you can use the "bounce test" against a flat surface.

20. Dong Quai

Dong Quai (Angelica Sinensis) is a plant. The root is used to manufacture medicines. Premenstrual syndrome (PMS), menopausal symptoms, and menstrual cramps can all be treated with Dong q uai. Additionally, it is taken orally for hypertension, infertility, joint discomfort, ulcers, "tired blood" (anemia), constipation, and to prevent and cure allergic reactions. Depigmentation of the skin and psoriasis are two more conditions that are treated with Dong Quai when taken orally. As part of a multi-ingredient preparation for treating premature ejaculation, some men apply Dong Quai on the skin of the penis.

Health Benefits Of Dong Quai

> ➤ **Physcial Health Of Women**

Strengthening the uterus, enhancing uterine tone, and regulating the menstrual cycle are just a few benefits of this effective women's herb. It can also manage estrogen levels that are either too high or too low. In Traditional Chinese Medicine (TCM), Dong q uai is also used as a blood tonic. Research has shown that Dong Quai increases red blood cells count, which is beneficial after menstruation has stopped since it speeds up the process of replenishing the blood. It is typically used for circumstances of stagnation, including PCOS, endometriosis, ovarian cysts, and uterine fibroids. It promotes blood flow to the reproductive system while reducing congestion and pain. When treating menopause symptoms in TCM, Dong Quai is typically prescribed along with other medicines.

> ➤ **Bone Wellness**

Osteoporosis, which particularly affects menopausal and post-menopausal women, may be a result of the sharp decline in estrogen levels that occurs with menopause. According to research, Dong Quai promotes the formation of new bones while also strengthening the existing ones. The herb Dong Quai enhances bone remodeling by increasing protein secretion and collagen synthesis of bone tissue when applied to osteoblast precursor cells, an important element involved in bone formation.

➢ Internal Health

This adaptable plant has also been found to have a gastroprotective function, guarding against excessive stomach acid in the layer of mucus that protects the digestive tract. Chronic gastrointestinal tract inflammation can result from the layer being damaged by too much stomach acid. Small tears will form in the small intestine and stomach if untreated. Peptic ulcer is the most popular name for them. Dong Quai has strong anti-inflammatory properties that can stop these lesions from ever developing. According to studies, it can also stop harm to the digestive tract's mucus lining up to 12 hours after consumption.

➢ Heart Wellness

Dong Quai can benefit heart health in two different ways. Firstly, it has active ingredients that lengthen the time between heartbeats and relax blood pressure in the arteries, both of which contribute to an increase in blood flow. Dong Quai may act as a preventive measure against atherosclerosis, myocardial infarction (heart attack), and hypertension because, according to research, it lessens the creation of plaque in the blood vessel walls. Secondly, studies on Dong Quai have shown that it lowers the risk levels of triglycerides and cholesterol. The risk of heart disease can be decreased, whereas heart's health can be improved by lowering cholesterol levels.

Side Effects

Dong Quai can increase the skin's sensitivity to the sun, which could lead to inflammation and burns. Those who consume Dong Quai should avoid direct sunlight or use enough sunscreen to prevent this.

Tips For Use

The plant is available in a variety of forms, and dosages also differ greatly. For example, a crude root extract via decoction can be taken daily in amounts ranging from 3 to 15 g, while formulations containing 75 mg to 500 mg can be taken up to six times daily.

How To Harvest Dong Quai

In order to use the root later as cut pieces or powder, it is picked in the fall or winter and dried.

21. Echinacea

A collection of blooming plants with the common name "Echinacea" are indigenous to North America. Echinacea, often known as purple coneflower, is one of the most well-liked plants in the world. For ages, Native Americans have utilized it to treat a variety of illnesses. It is best recognized today as a herbal over-the-counter treatment for the common cold or flu. These plants are also known as coneflowers. Depending on the species, the petals may be pink or purple and surround a seed head, or cone, that is prickly and dark brown or red.

There are three widely recognized varieties of Echinacea, which are components of herbal remedies:

- E. Angustifolia has little petals
- E. pallida, a flower with pale petals
- E. purpurea has purple petals

Health Benefits Of Echinacea

Echinacea supplements have different health benefits. These are:

> **Defend Against The Common Cold**

You may better fight off colds and the flu brought on by viruses or bacteria if you take echinacea to boost your immune system. The echinacea plant has compounds that, according to some studies, aid in the production of white blood cells in your body. These white blood cells assist your immune system in fighting illnesses when the nose, mouth, and throat (your upper respiratory tract) get infected.

> ### Cure Infections

Many different infections may be resistant to echinacea's effects. Echinacea can be used to treat ear infections, urinary tract infections, and cuts or wounds that take long to heal, according to research. While echinacea might occasionally aid in the disappearance of mild infections, you should visit your doctor if the issue persists.

> ### Cure Eczema

A lotion containing echinacea extract may be beneficial for those who suffer from eczema and skin inflammation. Daily application of echinacea cream helps strengthen the skin's outer layer of protection while also reducing eczema-related inflammation. It's still too early to tell whether echinacea helps most people with eczema, though. People with eczema frequently have allergies and asthma, so it's crucial to be aware of any potential allergic reactions.

Side Effects

Echinacea often has no negative side effects and may have health advantages. However, in rare circumstances, using echinacea supplements may come with some risks:

> ### Drug Interactions

Immunosuppressant-taking patients shouldn't take echinacea because it may interact with their medicine. This includes sufferers of any autoimmune disease, leukemia, diabetes, HIV, or tuberculosis. People who have had organ transplant are also included in this category.

> ### Responses To Allergies

Even though they are uncommon, allergic reactions can be brought on by echinacea. Echinacea can trigger anaphylaxis, even with mild reactions (loss of breathing). An increased risk exists for those who have asthma or other allergies. People who are allergic to members of the daisy family should take particular note of this. Before using echinacea, see your physician if you suffer from allergies or asthma.

Tips For Use

For echinacea, there isn't a currently approved dosage. Echinacea research results are very inconsistent, which is one factor. Additionally, echinacea products mostly do not contain what is indicated on the label. Because of this, only buy echinacea products from reputable manufacturers. The following doses, however, have been shown to be beneficial in boosting immunity, according to research:

- ✓ **Extract in dry powder:** Echinacea purpurea, three times each day, 300–500 mg.
- ✓ **Liquid-extract tinctures:** 2.5 ml administered three times daily, or as much as 10 ml.
- ✓ **Tea:** Boil 1 teaspoon of root in 1 to 2 cups of water for 10 minutes, or steep 1 to 2 teaspoons of leaf or flower in 1 cup of boiling water. However, it's essential to adhere to the directions provided with your particular supplement.

The long-term effects of echinacea on the body are still mostly understood, so these suggestions are for short-term use only.

How To Harvest Echinacea

The echinacea plant's roots and aerial parts are both useful. The roots of the plant contain the most potent medication, although the aerial parts are most freq uently utilized to make herbal drinks. The aerial sections can be harvested in the second year of growth.

Cutting the stem above the lowest pair of leaves is all that is necessary to collect the aerial sections. Leaves and flower buds should be separated from the stem and spread out to dry. Anytime during the growth season is suitable for doing this. It's an excellent time to do it when you are reducing the amount of echinacea. In spring or fall, take the roots of a plant that is 2-3 years old. While E. Augustifolia has taproot, E. Purpurea has fibrous roots. Lift the roots from the soil surrounding the Echinacea plant using a shovel or garden fork to collect it. You can now cut the root into pieces from the root ball or dig up the entire plant to get to the roots. You can thin out your echinacea patch by taking out the entire plant. You can replant the leftover roots in the ground if you only want to harvest a portion of the root ball.

22. Ginger

Ginger (Zingiber officinale) is highly valued in herbal medicine for alleviating nausea and indigestion. This traditional practice has been strongly supported by scientific inq uiry. Numerous human studies have demonstrated that ginger lowers nausea and vomiting brought on by chemotherapy, motion sickness, and pregnancy. According to a National Cancer Institute study, patients' nausea was decreased by an additional 40% if they had 0.5 to 1.0 g of ginger, in addition to antinausea drugs, for three days before and after chemotherapy. It is unclear how ginger reduces nausea, but current thought is that its molecules connect to receptors in the gastrointestinal tract, which then work to lessen nausea and speed up digestion, shortening the time food remains in the stomach. Research is being done on ginger's potential to lessen arthritic pain and inflammation. Human studies have demonstrated that ginger treats knee osteoarthritis pain more effectively than a placebo but not as effectively as ibuprofen.

Health Benefits Of Ginger

Here are some benefits:

> **Combats Germs**

Fresh ginger has certain chemical components that help your body fight off pathogens. They may also deter the spread of viruses, like RSV. They are particularly effective at stopping the growth of bacteria, such as E. coli and shigella.

> **Maintains Dental Health**

The antimicrobial properties of ginger may help enhance your smile. Gingerols, active substances found in ginger, prevent oral germs from proliferating. These same microorganisms can also result in periodontal disease, a dangerous gum infection.

➢ Reduces Nausea

Ginger is effective for calming an upset stomach, particularly during pregnancy. It might function by dissolving and eliminating gas that has accumulated in your intestines. Additionally, it might alleviate chemotherapy-related nausea or motion sickness.

➢ Pain Relief For Muscles

Ginger won't instantly relieve muscle discomfort, but it might ease soreness over time. According to some research, participants who took ginger the night after exercising and experiencing muscle aches felt reduced pain.

➢ Eases The Symptoms Of Arthritis

Since ginger has anti-inflammatory properties, it lessens edema. That could be especially beneficial for treating osteoarthritis and rheumatoid arthritis symptoms. You may be able to reduce discomfort and swelling by eating ginger orally or applying a ginger compress or patch to your skin.

- ➢ **Reduces Cancer Growth**

According to several researches, the bioactive compounds in ginger may help some malignancies, including colorectal, gastric, ovarian, liver, skin, breast, and prostate cancers, grow more slowly. However, more studies are required to find out if this is true.

Side Effects

The FDA views ginger as safe when used in moderation, but it does not support or control its use as a medication or dietary supplement. Consult a doctor before increasing the amount of ginger in your diet or using a ginger supplement. Some supplements can interfere with drugs or result in additional health issues.

Tips For Use

For fresh ginger tea, make a cup of fresh ginger tea by chopping up a 1-inch piece of fresh ginger rhizome. Simmer in two cups of water on low heat for 15 minutes. Drink one to three cups daily to improve circulation and treat coughs and colds. For dried ginger tea, boil one cup of water, add 1/4 to 1/2 teaspoon of ginger powder, and let simmer for 10 minutes. Throw away the powder and pour the tea. Drink one cup after meals to relieve nausea or bloating. For capsules, take 250–500 mg capsules two–three times daily. Concentrated extracts are frequently used to treat osteoarthritis. Apply as instructed.

How To Harvest Ginger

Rhizomes should be gently dug up for harvest. After that, trim the stems and thoroughly rinse the soil off. Rhizomes can either be harvested in batches or as needed.

23. Ginkgo

A big tree with leaves in the shape of fans is called a ginkgo (Ginkgo Biloba). For memory issues, the leaves are frequently ingested or incorporated in supplements. A herb with a high concentration of antioxidants called ginkgo biloba is used to improve brain function and treat a number of ailments. In existence for more than 200 million years, the ginkgo tree is one of the oldest living trees. Despite being a native of China, Japan, and Korea, it is now grown in both Europe and the United States.

It appears to increase blood flow and could function as an antioxidant to prevent the deterioration of the brain. It is freq uently used orally to treat anxiety, eyesight issues, memory and cognitive issues, and many other ailments. However, the majority of these applications lack strong scientific backing.

Health Benefits Of Ginkgo

Several health benefits of ginkgo biloba include the following:

> ➤ **Alzheimer's, Dementia, And Improved Memory**

Ginkgo may benefit those who are suffering from dementia, according to some data. Possible advantages are:

- Better memory and thinking
- Enhanced social skills
- Improved capacity to perform daily chores

EGb 761, an extract of ginkgo biloba, was found to be clinically effective in treating Alzheimer's dementia, according to one study. Ginkgo, according to researchers, boosts brain blood flow and shields the brain and other affected areas from neuronal loss, which is thought to enhance cognitive function.

> ➤ **Anxiety**

The ginkgo tree may help reduce anxiety's symptoms. According to a study, ginkgo users with generalized anxiety disorder felt less anxious than those who took a placebo. Ginkgo should not be used by those who take Xanax for anxiety, as it may lessen the medication's effectiveness.

> **Glaucoma**

In a short research, patients with glaucoma who took 120 milligrams of gingko daily for eight weeks saw improvements in their eyesight. According to a certain research, gingko may aid those with macular degeneration in maintaining their vision for a longer period.

Side Effects

Ginkgo leaf extract is probably safe for consumption by most people when taken orally. It may result in a few mild adverse effects, including nausea, headaches, lightheadedness, and allergic skin responses. There is some worry that ginkgo leaf extract may make you more susceptible to bleeding and bruising as well as arrhythmia. Taken internally, the roasted seed or raw ginkgo plant may be harmful. More than ten roasted seeds consumed everyday can have dangerous adverse effects, like seizures. Consuming fresh seeds might cause death. They are hazardous and poisonous. Also, there isn't enough information to determine whether ginkgo is safe when applied to the skin.

Tips For Use

The following types of ginkgo biloba are offered for sale:

✓ Capsules
✓ Tablets

✓ Fluid extracts

✓ Dried herbs or tea

One teaspoon of ginkgo leaf should be steeped in one cup of water for five to seven minutes to make tea. Aim for one to two cups per day. Follow the manufacturer's instructions or typically take 3 to 5 ml of the tincture twice daily. The majority of studies have used twice-daily dosages of 120 mg of extracts standardized to include between 24 and 27 percent flavone glycosides and between 6 and 7 percent triterpenes.

How To Harvest Ginkgo

Follow these steps to harvest ginkgo:

1. In the late summer to early October, keep an eye on the ginkgo tree's leaves. The fruit can be picked whenever the trees start to droop and change color. Additionally, the ripe ginkgo fruit releases an offensive odor.

2. Put on some rubber gloves before grabbing the ginkgo's fruit. Pull it from the tree by giving it a little twist. Ginkgo trees will also drop their ripe fruits. Keep an eye on the ground underneath you and pick up any ripe ginkgo that isn't partially eaten by animals.

3. The ginkgo fruit should be submerged in a pail of chilled water. Pull the ripe fruit apart and take the nuts out while still wearing gloves. Throw away the fruit and water. The nuts should be rinsed under a cool faucet to get rid of any bad smell left.

4. Before eating, boil the nuts for at least five to ten minutes. After straining the water, let the ginkgo nuts cool a little. Pull the nuts open with your fingers or a pair of pliers, then take the kernels out. The kernels can be eaten.

24. Ginseng

The herb ginseng (Panax ginseng) has been utilized for a number of medical conditions. It shouldn't be mixed up with other ginseng varieties. One of the several ginseng varieties freq uently utilized in herbal therapy is panax ginseng. East Asian highlands is home to the ginseng plant, and it is from these mountains that the ginseng consumed—often in teas and supplements—is gathered. Traditional Chinese medicine holds that each variety of ginseng has particular therapeutic benefits. For instance, it is reported that some varieties of Panax ginseng contain "warming" characteristics that may help blood flow.

Health Benefits of Ginseng

Panax ginseng, sometimes known as Asian or Korean ginseng, and American ginseng are the two primary varieties (Panax q uinq uefolius). According to studies, each kind has a uniq ue set of advantages. In contrast to the Asian version, American ginseng is regarded as less stimulating in traditional Chinese medicine. Even while many other plants, such as eleuthero or Siberian ginseng, go by the name of ginseng, they lack the ginsenosides compound that makes them effective. There are numerous medical ailments for which ginseng has traditionally been utilized although no thoughtful research has been done on its advantages for the majority of them. A few of these include:

➢ **Developing Resistance**

According to some research, ginseng may strengthen your immune system. There is some evidence that one form of American ginseng extract may lessen the frequency and severity of colds in adults.

➢ **Regulating Blood Sugar**

According to numerous human research, ginseng may reduce blood sugar levels.

> ➤ **Increasing Concentration**

There is some preliminary research that suggests ginseng may temporarily improve learning and concentration. Ginseng and an extract from the ginkgo tree leaves, another conventional treatment for dementia, have been combined in several investigations of mental performance. Even though these findings are fascinating, many professionals believe that we still need more proof.

Side Effects

Panax ginseng may be safely used when taken orally for up to six months. Taking Panax ginseng for longer than six months may be dangerous. When used over a prolonged period, it might have effects similar to those of hormones. Sleeping difficulty is the most freq uent side effect. There have been reports of uncommon adverse effects, such as severe rash, liver damage, and life-threatening allergic responses. There is insufficient trustworthy data to determine the safety of panax ginseng when applied to the skin. It could result in negative consequences, including burning and itchiness.

Tips for Use

Standardized Asian ginseng preparations with ginsenoside concentrations of 4–7 percent, taken daily in doses of 100–200 mg. One to two ml of tinctures should be used three times daily. In order to make tea, simmer three to six tablespoons of root in three to four cups of water for 45 minutes. One to three cups should be consumed each day after straining and cooling. As for capsule, 500 to 1,000 mg of dried, powdered root per capsule, should be taken once or twice a day.

How To Harvest Ginseng

Even commercially produced ginseng may only be harvested from mature plants (at least three years old) and only in the late summer and early fall.

Therefore, if you're thinking of growing ginseng, keep in mind that before your plants are ready to harvest and market, you'll need patience. Since ginseng outlives people, there is no need to rush a harvest. Use a shovel to carefully dig up your crop beginning no earlier than the fourth year of the plant to avoid damaging the roots. Rinse your ginseng gently to remove any dirt, and then dry it in a cool, dry area with plenty of airflow. Turning the roots daily may hasten the drying process and avoid mold in larger roots, which might take several weeks to dry.

25. Goldenseal

Goldenseal (Hydrastis Canadensis) is a North American herb. Historically, Native Americans utilized goldenseal to cure a wide range of health issues, such as sore or itchy eyes, mouth ulcers, and even tuberculosis. Yellow root is another term for goldenseal. Its brown and yellow roots give goldenseal its name. Small blooms, crinkly 5-lobed leaves, and a small fruit make up the remainder of the plant.

Health Benefits Of Goldenseal

Among the health benefits of goldenseal are:

➢ **Eye Support With Antibiotics**

Goldenseal is a typical element in herbal eyewashes to relieve itching
from seasonal allergies or discomfort from eye infections. According
to one study, taking excessive levels of berberine, one of the bacteria-

killing antimicrobial substances found in goldenseal, may harm the cells that line the surface of the eye lens. Goldenseal for the eyes is generally used in safer dosages, although users should still be cautious, especially in bright sunshine. According to studies, this effect on the eyes is not caused by ingesting goldenseal orally.

➤ Heart Wellness

Due to the active components of goldenseal, especially its star phytonutrient "berberine," the heart is well-protected and supported. Arrhythmias and heart palpitations can be treated with berberine, which also helps maintain normal heart rhythm.

According to studies, berberine "prolongs the length of ventricular action potential" and possesses anti-arrhythmic characteristics. This transient voltage change across the cell membrane of heart cells is also known as a "cardiac action potential." The cardiovascular effects of berberine "indicate its probable clinical value in the treatment of arrhythmias and/or heart failure," according to the study's conclusion. Additionally, it possesses vasodilating qualities, which relaxes and widens the blood vessels and maintains normal blood pressure.

➤ Skin Wellness

Goldenseal can be used to treat skin conditions, like acne, eczema, and psoriasis, because it has potent antioxidant and anti-microbial effects. Additionally, ringworm, herpes, blisters, and sores have all been successfully treated with it. Goldenseal can be used as a poultice to apply directly to problem areas or as a component in lotions, salves, and ointments. Goldenseal is excellent at both cleaning and healing wounds, and it can be used instead of harsher skin disinfectants to gently clean cuts and bruises and hasten recovery.

➤ It Might Aid In Preventing Urinary Tract Infections

Urinary tract infections may be avoided by the substance berberine because it may stop bacteria from adhering to the lining of the urethra and bladder. To be sure, further research on goldenseal is required, as with a number of other claims.

➤ Broad-Based Immune Support

Berberine and hydrastine, two of the alkaloids found in goldenseal, appear to promote immunological function. They are antimicrobial in the sense that they eradicate microorganisms and might potentially inhibit the development of malignancies. These substances may also lessen inflammation, which further explains how they could aid in relieving gastrointestinal pain and cold-related symptoms like a sore throat.

Side Effects

Nausea, impaired liver function, and vomiting are examples of possible adverse effects.

Tips For Use

There isn't any research that points to the optimal goldenseal dosages. Given the variety of forms that goldenseal supplements take, doses can change. The recommended dosage for your vitamin may look something like this:

- ✓ Vitamins made from dried goldenseal roots: a typical dosage is three times daily, 0.5 to 10 grams.
- ✓ Turpentine and liquid extract of goldenseal: three times per day, in the range of 0.3 to 10 ml.
- ✓ Goldenseal tea: typically two teaspoons of the dry herb are steeped in one cup of boiling water for at least 15 minutes.

How To Harvest Goldenseal

Goldenseal plants are harvested or divided when they have fully colonized the land they were planted in, typically in four to five years. The plants will begin to crowd one another if nothing is done, and the oldest roots will finally die. When the tips have died back in fall, start digging roots. Harvest the leaves and stems in early fall while the foliage is still green if there is a market for them. Dig gently, preserving all the fibrous roots. With a fork, small plots can be dug. A motorized digger of some sort will be necessary for large fields. Diggers for potatoes, horseradish, and bulbs have been modified. For replanting, choose robust, healthy plants and have a container on hand to keep them cold and wet, or prepare beds for rapid replanting.

26. Grapes

Grape plants (Vitis Venifera) is a fruit-bearing vines from the Vitaceae family. They have been around for so long that fossilized leaves, stems, and seeds have been discovered in deposits from the Northern hemisphere's Neogene and Paleogene periods, which span a period of between 2.6 and 65 million years ago.

Whether they are blue, purple, red, pink, green, or amber in hue, their vibrant globe-like, juicy, sugary berries are what we refer to as grapes. Grapes are a powerhouse of nutrients. They contain high amounts of vitamin C, a potent antioxidant important for the development of connective tissue, immune system function, and wound healing. They also include potassium, which is necessary for healthy kidney and heart function, muscular contraction, and nerve signal transmission, as well as vitamin K, which aids in blood clotting and maintenaning strong bones.

Health Benefits Of Grapes

Vitamins, minerals, and antioxidants are abundant in grapes. They contain a lot of water as well, which can help you stay hydrated. Here are some health benefits of eating grapes.

➢ Eliminates Cancer

Grapes, which are rich in antioxidants, may aid in the battle against free radicals, chemicals that can harm cells and perhaps cause cancer. Resveratrol, an antioxidant found in grapes, may prevent cancer by lowering inflammation and preventing the development of cancer cells. In addition to these antioxidants, grapes also include q uercetin, anthocyanins, and catechins, which together may be particularly effective against cancer.

➢ Lowers Blood Pressure

The salt content in grapes is extremely low. They work well with a low-sodium diet regimen that lowers blood pressure. Potassium, which is abundant in grapes and can also help regulate blood pressure, is another healthy nutrient. Low potassium consumption may increase your risk of high blood pressure.

➢ Prevents Heart Disease

It's possible that resveratrol does more than just fight cancer. Additionally, it has been demonstrated to aid in heart disease defense. According to one study, people with diets higher in potassium than sodium had a lower risk of dying from heart disease than those with diets lower in potassium.

> ## Lowers High Cholesterol

Grapes have a lot of fiber, which makes them a fantastic choice for lowering high cholesterol. In a study of individuals with high cholesterol, those who consumed three cups of red grapes each day for eight weeks had decreased total cholesterol.

> ## Reduces The Risk Of Diabetes

Due to their low glycemic index, grapes won't cause a spike in blood sugar levels. According to studies, grape components may raise insulin sensitivity and lower blood sugar levels, which may improve how well your body uses glucose.

> ## Enhances Sleep

Having trouble sleeping soundly at night? A small amount of melatonin is present in grapes. They don't have many calories and may aid in your ability to sleep.

Side Effects

The presence of vitamin K in grapes may alter how blood thinners like warfarin (Coumadin) function in your body. Instead of avoiding grapes and other foods high in vitamin K, attempt to maintain a daily vitamin K consumption that is about constant. If you are taking a blood thinner, you should also let your doctor know about your eating habits and any supplements you are taking, such as grape seed extract.

Tips For Use

It can be used for the following:

- ✓ **Wine:** One serving of wine per day is recommended for women; for men it's one to two.
- ✓ **Grape juice:** Four to six ounces of dark purple grape juice should be consumed every day.
- ✓ **Grape seed extract:** 300 to 600 mg daily.

How To Harvest Grapes

With one hand holding a cluster of grapes, use sharp garden shears or pruners to cut the entire cluster off the vine. It is recommended to use a sharp cutting tool because breaking off the cluster will harm the plant and be tough. Each cluster should be placed delicately in a pail or bucket.

27. Licorice

The herb called licorice (Glycyrrhiza glabra) thrives in some regions of Asia and Europe. Licorice is known to include compounds that lower swelling and coughing and boost the body's natural ability to heal ulcers. Many American-made "licorice" items don't actually include licorice. They contain anise oil, which has a "black licorice"-like flavor and aroma. There are numerous illnesses for which licorice is utilized, including mouth sores, liver edema, and eczema, although the majority of these applications lack solid scientific backing.

Health Benefits Of Licorice

These are licorice's health benefits:

> **Infection And Skin Inflammation**

Licorice root contains a variety of chemicals that may aid to lessen inflammation in the skin and other bodily tissues. Several skin disorders can be treated with the aid of these substances. According to research, licorice root glycyrrhizin extract may help with eczema symptoms.

➢ Hepatitis C

The liver-infecting hepatitis C virus may be treated with glycorrhizin. Hepatitis C can result in inflammation and long-term liver damage if left untreated. According to studies, glycyrrhizin exhibits antimicrobial action against hepatitis C in cell samples, suggesting that it may one day be used as a therapy for this virus.

➢ Decayed Teeth

According to several studies, licorice extract may help fight oral germs that cause tooth decay. Streptococcus mutans bacteria might grow more slowly in the mouth when licorice root extract is used. As a result, the environment around the teeth becomes less acidic, which reduces the risk of developing dental cavities.

➢ Throat Pain

Various licorice varieties may be used to treat upper respiratory conditions like sore throats. Most people assert that licorice root tea reduces mild discomfort and eases sore throats. Additionally, studies have demonstrated the beneficial effects of several licorice formulations in clinical situations. Asthma symptoms may also be lessened using herbal treatmentscontaining licorice root.

Side Effects

Licorice is probably safe for the majority of people when consumed in conventional dietary portions. When used in dosages of up to 4.5 grams per day for up to four months, the licorice that has had the chemical glycyrrhizin removed may be safe. Glycyrrhizin-containing licorice may be harmful if ingested in large doses or over an extended period. For several weeks, consuming five grams or more of licorice daily can have serious negative effects, including heart attack. It affects people more readily if they have heart illness, kidney problems, or high blood pressure. Large doses of licorice in candies, lozenges or tea may potentially have negative side effects. Gel containing 2% licorice root extract can be used topically for up to two weeks without any risk. Licorice can conceivably be used safely for up to a week with a mouthwash.

Tips For Use

In addition to chewable tablets, licorice is also offered as a liq uid extract, capsules, powder, and loose herb. Licorice has a wide range of medical uses that people might employ, including:

- ✓ Eczema can be treated by combining the herb with a skin-friendly gel, such as aloe vera gel.
- ✓ Tea for a sore throat is made by steeping loose herbs in boiling water.
- ✓ For the treatment of ulcers, one might sublingually or orally administer liquid licorice extract.
- ✓ Using chewable licorice tablets and capsules.

Without previously seeing a doctor, people should not regularly eat licorice sweets, drinks, or supplements.

How To Harvest Licorice Root

The optimum time to collect licorice roots is in fall after the growing season has ended and plants have done flowering. Licorice roots can be gathered when the plant is two years old. Given the size of licorice root, you'll need to dig up the entire plant, including the roots. Either a spade or a garden fork can be used to lift the entire plant out of the ground. Garden shears should be used to trim and thoroughly wash the roots. If you want to replant the plant in your garden, you can leave the tap root and a few of the main roots on it.

28. Hops

The hop blossom (humulus lupulus) is what is used to make beer. The word "hops" derives from the Anglo-Saxon verb "to climb," "hopper." Numerous compounds, including bitter acids, are present in hops and contribute to their bitter flavor. Some of the compounds in hops appear to work similarly to the estrogen hormone, while others seem to make people drowsy. People frequently use hops to treat a variety of illnesses, including anxiety, insomnia, restlessness, and menopause symptoms, among many others.

Health Benefits Of Hops

For more than 2,000 years, the hops blossom has been used medicinally to treat a number of conditions. Though still in its early stages, contemporary research supports hops' ability to aid with mood, relaxation, and other things. This is probably due to the flower's abundance of polyphenols, antioxidants, and advantageous essential oils, including linalool, which reduces oxidative stress. Recent studies suggest that hops may be beneficial for the following conditions because of the substances they contain:

➢ **May Aid In Sleep**

Hops are renowned for being relaxing. Hops may help if you have difficulties falling asleep or a crazy schedule that interferes with your circadian rhythm, commonly known as your sleep-wake cycle. It might help people feel happier. Hops can also improve your mood.

➤ Could Alleviate Hot Flashes

According to a different study, hops may also aid with hot flashes and other menopausal symptoms. Hops contain a flavonoid called 8-prenylnaringenin, a phytoestrogen that may mimic the effects of estrogen in the body. More research is req uired on this subject to evaluate the safety of long-term dosage.

➤ May Boost the Immune System

Hops contain a flavonoid molecule called xanthohumol, which is thought to potentially have antiviral, anti-clotting, anti-inflammatory, and even anti-tumor properties.

Potential Side Effects

Hops supplements are thought to be safe and have few adverse effects when taken for health reasons. The effects of this symptom are typically lessened by taking the herbal supplement right before bed. Hops should be avoided by several populations, especially thedepressed since they may worsen their symptoms. Hops should be avoided by those with endometriosis, gynecomastia (enlarged male breasts), and some kinds of breast cancer because of their estrogen-like activity. Hops supplements should be stopped two weeks before surgery since they have a sedative effect and could intensify the effects of anesthetic. You should refrain from combining hops with other CNS depressants, like alcohol, sleeping medications, or caffeine, for the same reason.

Tips For Use

You can use hops for the following:

- ✓ **Tea:** Let one cup of water and one teaspoon of female hops strobiles steep for five to seven minutes. Add honey to taste. Drink it before going to sleep.
- ✓ **Capsules:** Take 500 mg, 1–3 times per day with valerian root.
- ✓ **Tincture:** Take 2 ml of tincture, 1-3 times per day.

How To Harvest Hops

Hops can be harvested in two different ways: manually (preferred for first-year harvests) or by cutting the bine (recommended for all harvests after the first year). To protect the root system and crown, cut the bine two to three feet above the ground if you must chop it down. When picking cones from first-year bines, try to wait until the bine dies out before cutting it down. The root system will receive essential nutrients that will help it survive the winter. Trim the bine to prevent injury to or contamination of the valuable lupulin glands in the upcoming years. Each mature plant should yield one to two pounds of dried hops. When harvesting hops, be sure to put on sturdy, abrasion-resistant clothing, gloves, and goggles. Hooked hairs on hops can result in skin rashes and minor wounds.

29. Parsley

The flowering herb parsley (Petroselinum crispum), a member of the Apiaceae family, is widely farmed. It is widely used in Middle Eastern,

European, and American cuisine. Fresh parsley comes in two varieties, both of which are regularly found in markets and other food stores. Their descriptive names, curly leaf parsley and flat leaf parsley, are how most people who are familiar with them call them. French parsley, also known as curly leaf parsley, is freq uently used as a garnish. Italian parsley, also known as flat leaf parsley, is used more freq uently as a salad and cooked food ingredient since it has a stronger flavor.

Health Benefits Of Parsley

Numerous vitamins, minerals, and antioxidants found in parsley have significant positive effects on health. It has a particularly high vitamin K content. More than 70% of the daily necessary amount of parsley is present in just one tablespoon of freshly chopped parsley. Additionally, parsley is a strong source of vitamin A and flavonoids, which are anti-oxidants. The other health benefits of parsley include:

➢ **To Prevent Cancer**

Apigenin, a flavone, is present in parsley in considerable amounts. While other health advantages of parsley may be diminished by heating and/or drying, apigenin content is increased. The best source of apigenin in nature is dried parsley. The pigments in some blooming plants called flavones are potent antioxidants. As an anticancer drug, apigenin has particularly promising potential.

➢ **Diuresis**

The process of diuresis is when your kidneys produce more urine than usual to flush something out of your body. Parsley has potent natural diuretic properties and helps lower blood pressure and bloating.

➢ **Healthy Bones**

The vitamin K content of parsley has been connected to the health of bones. Both bone mineral density and development are supported by the vitamin. According to one study, parsley was discovered to help protect against osteoporosis in rats.

> **Eye Care**

Lutein and zeaxanthin, two antioxidants that help prevent age-related macular degeneration, are both found in parsley together with vitamin A, which supports eye surface protection.

Side Effects

When parsley oil is consumed, it can cause headaches, euphoria, dizziness, loss of balance, convulsions, and kidney damage. Parsley cutters have been seen to have photodermatitis in response to the psoralen chemicals contained in parsley.

Tips For Use

Parsley is used for the following:

- ✓ **Food:** Parsley is a fresh or dried herb used in dishes across many cultures. It is first and foremost a food. For instance, the urinary tract requires roughly 6 g of parsley leaves or roots daily.
- ✓ **Tincture:** Typically, parsley tinctures, or alcohol extracts of the herb, are dosed at 1 to 2 ml, three times a day.
- ✓ **Capsule:** 450 to 900 mg of parsley leaf per capsule, up to three times daily.
- ✓ **Tea:** Place 1/4 cup (or two to three teaspoons) of fresh parsley leaves in a cup of boiling water. Allow to stand for five minutes, strain, and consume up to three times per day. If desired, tea can be sweetened.

How To Harvest Parsley

When you harvest, only take what you need. Just snip off one, two, or three stems, and your plant will continue to produce parsley all season long. Don't trim the plant all the way back or remove it.

30. Pomegranate

Pomegranates (Punica granatum) are round, crimson fruits. They have a white interior flesh heavily populated with crunchy, juicy edible seeds known as arils. Pomegranate is a fruit with a thick skin that is sweet and sour. The thousands of juicy seeds inside the non-edible skin can be eaten alone or added to salads, oats, hummus, and other foods. Pomegranates are cultivated on trees. To produce and ripen these tough, delectable fruits, the trees req uire sufficient heat.

Health Benefits Of Pomegranate

Compared to green tea or red wine, pomegranates can have up to three times more antioxidants. Antioxidants shield cells from harm, guard against illnesses, like cancer, and lessen inflammation and signs of aging. Pomegranates also have the following additional health benefits:

➢ A Healthy Heart

Pomegranates may protect the heart in a variety of ways, according to studies, including by lowering blood pressure and blood sugar levels. A prominent cause of heart disease is atherosclerosis, which is the accumulation of cholesterol and lipids in the arteries. Pomegranate juice might assist in lowering low-density lipoprotein cholesterol, also known as "bad" cholesterol, which clogs arteries. It may also raise levels of high-density lipoprotein cholesterol, or "good" cholesterol, which reduces the risk of heart attacks and strokes.

➢ Control Of Diabetes

According to preliminary research, persons with type 2 diabetes who started drinking pomegranate juice experienced lessened insulin resistance. Pomegranates can also assist those who do not have diabetes in keeping a healthy weight.

> ### Reducing The Risk Of Cancer

Pomegranates are abundant in flavonoids and antioxidants, both of which are proven to protect your cells from damage by free radicals. According to some research, pomegranates may be useful in avoiding prostate, breast, lung, and colon cancer. Pomegranates may protect the heart in a variety of ways, according to studies, including by lowering blood pressure and blood sugar levels. Heart disease is frequently brought on by atherosclerosis, which is the accumulation of fat and cholesterol in the arteries. Low-density lipoprotein cholesterol, or "bad" cholesterol, which clogs arteries, may be lessened by pomegranate juice. Additionally, it can raise high-density lipoprotein cholesterol, also known as "good" cholesterol, which reduces the risk of heart attacks and strokes.

Side Effects Of Consuming Pomegranate Seeds

Although pomegranate seeds are probably safe, some people may have adverse reactions. They may develop an allergy to pomegranate fruits. Itching, swelling, a runny nose, and breathing difficulties are all indicators of an allergy.

The pomegranate's root, stem, or peel should not be eaten in large q uantities due to the toxin it may carry. The best course of action is to discuss any potential side effects with your doctor.

Tips For Use

✓ **Juice:** Eight ounces of juice every day.

✓ **Capsules:** Take 2 to 3 grams of powdered pomegranate capsules every day, on average.

How To Harvest Pomegranate

When it is time to harvest, cut the fruit off the tree rather than pull it off. Cut the fruit as near to the branch as you can while keeping the fruit's stem.

31. Sage

Sage is a herb. Sage comes in a variety of species. Common sage (Salvia officinalis) and Spanish sage are the two most popular types (Salvia lavandulaefolia). Sage is a member of the mint family and it's often used sparingly due to its potent flavor. Herbs, like oregano, rosemary, basil, and thyme, are also members of this family. Chemical abnormalities in the brain that impair memory and thought processes may be treated with sage. Additionally, it might alter how the body uses sugar and insulin.

Health Benefits Of Sage

Sage contains essential elements, like magnesium, zinc, and copper, in addition to a high concentration of vitamin K. Sage has many health benefits, including:

➢ Antioxidant Benefits

Antioxidants support the body's defense against free radicals, which can harm our cells and cause cancer. Vitamins A, C, and E, which are antioxidants, are present in trace amounts in sage. Additionally, it contains more than 160 different kinds of polyphenols, another plant-based antioxidant. There are several different acidic chemicals in sage that also function as antioxidants. Rutin, chlorogenic acid, caffeic acid, rosmarinic acid, ellagic acid, and rosmarinic acid have all been associated with such advantages like lowered cancer risk, enhanced memory, and improved brain function.

Sage tea use increases antioxidant defense while also reducing LDL, or "bad" cholesterol. These advantages, as well as a rise in levels of beneficial cholesterol, were observed in subjects who drank two cups of sage tea each day.

➢ Oral Fitness

It has been demonstrated that sage possesses antibacterial properties that help kill plaq ue. According to a study, a mouthwash using sage as an ingredient effectively eradicates the Streptococcus mutans bacteria that causes cavities. Sage essential oil prevents the spread of the Candida albicans fungus and kills it.

➢ May Reduce Menopause Symptoms

During menopause, the body's estrogen levels normally decrease. The side effects of that decline include hot flushes, excessive perspiration, a dry vagina, and irritation. Traditional medicine has relied on sage to lessen these symptoms. Sage has estrogen-like characteristics that allow it to connect to specific brain receptors and reduce symptoms, such as hot flashes and excessive sweating. This may explain why it is useful in this situation. One study found that taking a sage supplement for eight weeks significantly reduced the amount of hot flashes experienced by participants.

➢ Could Aid In Blood Sugar Control

Studies support the use of sage leaves as a diabetic treatment that has been practiced traditionally. Sage leaf extract has been found to reduce blood sugar and enhance insulin sensitivity in human tests, much to the anti-diabetes medication rosiglitazone. Before sage extract can be suggested as a human diabetic medication, more research must be done.

Side Effects

When taken in usual meal levels, sage is LIKELY SAFE. When used topically or eaten orally in small doses for short periods, it is POSSIBLY SAFE (up to four months). Sage, however, may be dangerous if taken orally in high dosages or over an extended period.

A substance called thujone is present in some sage species, including common sage (Salvia officinalis). If you consume enough thujone, you could die. This substance has the potential to harm the liver, nervous system, and induce seizures.

Tips For Use

Below are tips on how to use Sage:

- ✓ **Tea:** Boil a cup of water with one teaspoon of finely chopped sage for 10 minutes. For a sore throat, consume or gargle.
- ✓ **Capsule:** Sage leaf 500 mg capsule, used twice day.
- ✓ **Tincture:** Take 2 ml, twice daily, or as directed by the manufacturer. To use as a gargle three times a day, mix 5 ml of tincture with a cup of water.

How To Harvest Sage

You can harvest sage by following these tips:

- Cut little sprigs or leaves from the plant by pinching them off.
- Harvest sparingly the first year to allow the plant to develop fully.

- Make sure to leave a few stalks after the first year so that the plant can rebloom later.

- One plant can be harvested up to three times in a season if it is well-established.

- Harvesting should cease in fall so that the plant can get ready for winter.

32. Psyllium

The seeds of Plantago ovata, a plant mostly produced in India, are the source of psyllium, a soluble fiber. People take psyllium as a nutritional supplement. Husk, granules, capsules, and powder are the different forms it can take. Additionally, manufacturers may add psyllium to baked goods and morning cereals. Psyllium husk is the primary active component in Metamucil, a fiber supplement that eases constipation. Psyllium can absorb water, thanks to its high solubility, and transform into a thick, viscous substance that hinders digestion in the small intestines.

Health Benefits Of Psyllium

The health benefits of psyllium are as follows:

➢ It Can Help With Digestion

Psyllium is thought to have "prebiotic potential," which implies that it promotes the development of healthy bacteria in your gut. It also has a lot of fiber, which helps with digestion.

➢ It Can Support The Development Of Immunity

It can assist your body in reducing inflammation, warding off infections, and promoting healthy cell and tissue growth because it is a prebiotic, and beneficial bacteria are crucial for improving your immunity.

➢ It Can Aid In Preventing Diarrhea

As a bulking agent, psyllium can help alleviate diarrhea. This indicates that psyllium powder expands and swells when a liq uid is introduced to it. The feces becomes harder and can transit more slowly as a result of absorbing water in the digestive system.

➢ It Can Help Treat Constipation

It can successfully relieve constipation because of its high fiber content. It acts as a laxative by absorbing fluids in the intestines, swelling, and forming a bulky stool that is simple to pass.

➢ It Can Help Lower The Risk Of Heart Disease

A diet rich in soluble fibers, such as psyllium, may help lower cholesterol and triglycerides and the risk of cardiovascular disease.

➢ It Can Aid In Weight Control

Fiber prolongs your feeling of fullness, which naturally reduces how much food you eat.

➢ It Can Aid In Blood Sugar Regulation

Psyllium fiber can aid in better blood sugar management. For people with diabetes, this can be q uite advantageous.

Side Effects Of Psyllium

Those who supplement their diets with psyllium may first have a few small side effects, but these normally go away after a week or so once the digestive system has adjusted to the additional fiber. They are as follows:

- Stomach pains

- Constipation

- Flatulence

Always read the manufacturer's label before ingesting supplements or over-the-counter laxatives. Stop using the product and call your doctor if you have any serious symptoms.

Tips For Use

For adults, it is advisable to take two to three tablespoons daily, divided between before breakfast and supper. Drink a full glass of water after mixing each dose, stirring it thoroughly, and then sipping another glass. Children (under the age of 18) should typically consume between one and two tablespoons depending on a child's age and size.

How To Harvest Psyllium

When fully mature, the lower leaves of psyllium flower spikes get dry and reddish brown, and the higher leaves turn yellow. The crop is picked in the morning after the dew has dried, which helps reduce shattering and field losses. At a height of 15 cm above the ground, mature plants are cut and then bound. A few days are given for them to dry before being thrashed.

33. Soybean

In East Asia, the legume known as soybean (Glycine max) is used to make a variety of products. It can be found in a wide range of foods, such as milk, tofu, and processed goods, like bread and cereals. Given that soybean contains all nine essential amino acids, which serve as the building block of proteins, it is most freq uently consumed as a plant protein. Additionally, it's regarded as a good source of fiber, potassium, magnesium, copper, manganese, calcium, and polyunsaturated fatty acids, like omega-3 and omega-6. Soybeans are available as supplements, such as tablets and powders, in addition to full foods.

Health Benefits Of Soybean

Soybeans have a variety of health benefits like other complete foods:

> **Cardiovascular Diet**

In soybeans, only 10%–15% of the total fat is saturated. This sort of fat, which often solidifies at room temperature, and may increase your risk of heart disease, is considerably more prevalent in other protein sources, such as ground beef or pork chops. Your ticker may benefit if you replace your meat meals with soy items, like tofu.

> ## The Healthy Fats

Important omega-6 and omega-3 fats are among the polyunsaturated fats that make up the majority of soy's fat content. Including those in a balanced diet may benefit your heart and reduce your risk of developing certain conditions. The following foods also contain healthy fats: nuts, seeds, fish, and vegetable oils.

> ## Has No Cholesterol

Foods made from soy are inherently cholesterol-free, just like all fruits, vegetables, and grains. Numerous studies appear to support the idea that merely consuming more soy protein can help reduce LDL, or "bad" cholesterol by 4%–6%.

> ## More Fiber

The amount of fiber in a cup of soybeans is around 10 grams. In contrast, animal proteins, like steak, poultry, and fish, have zero grams of protein. Additionally, soy contains a lot of fiber, which aids with regular bowel movements and may lessen the cholesterol you consume from other foods.

> ## Lowering Blood Pressure

Making soy a regular part of your diet may aid in preventing hypertension, often known as high blood pressure. In the beginning, soy contains a lot of proteins but little carbohydrates, a combination that tends to help lower blood pressure. Additionally, the soy itself might assist in lowering systolic blood pressure.

Side Effects

There are no negative conseq uences from consuming whole soy foods in moderation (a few times per week) if you do not have a soy allergy. Because of its nutritional composition, you can boost your protein intake while consuming fewer saturated fats, which will benefit your overall health. It is now considered that soy products do not raise the incidence of gynecological cancers in women, despite some of the isoflavones (also known as phytoestrogens) found in soy having estrogen-like properties. Furthermore, there is evidence to suggest that eating foods containing soy may actually reduce the incidence of breast cancer, particularly for women who reside in Asian nations where soy consumption is higher than in the United States. Men can consume soy products in moderation withoutany harm. Although estrogen is produced by both men and women, the former generate less of this hormone.

Tips For Use

A balanced diet need to contain soy products. Focus on edamame, soy nuts, miso, and tempeh rather than manufactured soy "junk" food.

Soy isoflavone extracts: Take 50 to 90 mg per day.

How To Harvest Soybeans

To harvest your soybean, follow these tips:

- Harvest soybeans when they are two to three inches (5-7 cm) long, green, full, and plump, or approximately half-mature, for green shell beans.
- After planting, soybeans take 45 to 65 days to reach harvest in readiness for shelling and fresh consumption.
- Dry soybeans need at least 100 days to reach harvest.
- Soybeans mature all at once; harvest the entire plant, then hang it upside down to dry.
- Shell soybeans' pods when they are completely dry.

34. Saw Palmetto

The saw palmetto (Serenoa repens) can reach a height of ten feet and has fan-shaped leaves with thorns. The fruit is used to make medicine when ripe. Saw palmetto appears to lessen the pressure on males' urine-transporting tubes. Additionally, saw palmetto may stop the conversion of testosterone into the more powerful form known as dihydrotestosterone (DHT). DHT levels being lower may aid in preventing some types of hair loss.

Health Benefits Of Saw Palmetto

The health benefits of saw palmetto are as follows:

> **It Supports Prostate Health**

Men's little prostate gland, which is situated between the bladder and penis, looks after sperm health. According to some research, saw palmetto might help maintain prostate health and prevent problems, like BPH and prostate cancer. Saw palmetto has been proven to be effective in the treatment of benign prostatic hyperplasia (BPH), a disorder that causes a gradual, noncancerous, yet abnormal growth of the prostate. Up to 75% of older men or men in their 70s, are affected by BPH. The prostate can become so huge that it prevents a person from completely emptying their bladder if not treated.

> ## Enhances Urinary Tract Performance

Older men frequently experience urinary tract symptoms, which might include incontinence and difficulties urinating. Saw palmetto may alleviate the urinary symptoms of benign prostatic hyperplasia (BPH), a disorder that causes the prostate gland to expand and impair the flow of urine. According to a study, taking 160 mg of saw palmetto twice a day for six months reduced lower urinary tract symptoms, increased urine flow, and enhanced general q uality of life.

> ## Can Prevent Male Pattern Baldness

Saw palmetto may aid in preventing androgenic alopecia, often known as male and female pattern baldness, which affects both sexes. It functions by inhibiting the enzyme that turns testosterone into dihydrotestosterone (DHT), an androgen-like hormone thought to be the root cause of this type of hair loss. It is believed that higher levels of androgen hormones, such as DHT, reduce the hair growth cycle and cause the development of shorter and thinner strands of hair.

➤ **Could Lessen Inflammation**

The anti-oxidants epicatechin and methyl gallate, which guard against chronic diseases and stop cell deterioration, are found in saw palmetto. Numerous studies suggest that saw palmetto may have anti-inflammatory q ualities, which may be useful in the treatment of some illnesses.

➤ **It Could Support The Control Of Testosterone Levels**

Men who want to increase their testosterone naturally frequently use saw palmetto. In addition to body composition, sex desire, mood, and cognition, testosterone regulation can impact a number of health-related factors. Age-related declines in testosterone levels are shown in certain studies, and low testosterone levels have been linked to such diseases as heart disease.

For the purpose of maintaining testosterone levels in the body, saw palmetto supplements work by reducing the activity of the enzyme 5α -R, which converts testosterone into dihydrotestosterone (DHT), another sex hormone.

Side Effects Of Saw Palmetto

Saw palmetto is typically regarded as safe and has sometimes been linked to negative side effects. In scientific studies, the most often reported saw palmetto adverse effects include poor breath, constipation, diarrhea, exhaustion, headache, nausea, stomach pain, and vomiting. Men who take saw palmetto have also complained of changes in their sexual desire, breast discomfort or enlargement, and erectile problems. Saw palmetto may affect the levels of sex hormones like estrogen and testosterone, albeit this hasn't been clearly shown in humans. As a result, before using saw palmetto, individuals with hormone-sensitive illnesses, such as breast cancer and prostate cancer, should speak with their doctors. Please note that saw palmetto is not suggested for everyone. Saw palmetto should be avoided by all women, especially by those who are expectant or nursing since it may affect the hormone levels. Saw palmetto may also not be suitable for people using hormonal contraceptives or hormone replacement therapy because it may change the hormone levels.

Tips for Use

Below are tips on how to use saw palmetto:

- ✓ **Extract:** Specific extracts, dosed at 160 mg twice daily, have been employed in studies. These extracts were standardized to include 80 to 90 percent fatty acids and sterols, the substances most effective for treating BPH symptoms.
- ✓ **Tincture:** One to two milliliters, three times daily.
- ✓ **Capsule:** Apply the manufacturer's instructions while taking capsules.

How To Harvest Saw Palmetto

If you catch your clothing on the saw-like teeth on the leaf stalks, you risk ripping it to pieces. To protect your hands from the cutting teeth on the leaf stalks, it is better to harvest using sturdy gloves. Large stalks carrying the fruits are hidden beneath the foliage.

35. Stevia

Stevia (Stevia rebaudiana) is the name given to a South American native herb with green leaves that has been used for centuries due to its incredibly sweet leaves. The active ingredients that give stevia its sweetness are largely stevioside and rebaudioside. In recent years, stevia has gained notoriety for being a sweetener that is more than 40 times sweeter than sugar without affecting blood sugar levels. In addition, unlike regular sugar, it has no harmful side effects on the body and is advantageous, especially for diabetics. The Asteraceae family, which includes sunflowers, contains more than 240 species of shrubs and tiny flowering plants.

Health Benefits Of Stevia

Stevia can help you control diabetes, lose weight, take care of your skin, and many other things. Let's go through some of its health benefits in more depth.

➤ It Helps With Weight Loss

Depending on the concentration of certain extracts in the species type, stevia may have few calories and be 40–300 times sweeter than sugar. As a result, consumers can eat stevia-sweetened items, like cakes, cookies, and candies, without having to worry about consuming too many calories from sugar, which improves their chances of effectively losing weight. This can also aid in reducing the amount of excess sugar in children's diets.

➤ Can Control Blood Pressure

Although stevioside is a particular kind of glycoside, there are other glycosides in stevia that can really relax blood vessels, stimulate urine, and aid in the body's ability to eliminate sodium. As a result, the cardiovascular system is less stressed, and blood pressure may decrease. This safeguards the heart's health and wards against ailments, like atherosclerosis, heart attack, and stroke.

> **Reduced Cholesterol Levels**

According to studies, consuming stevia significantly lowers levels of the bad LDL cholesterol and triglycerides while raising levels of the good HDL cholesterol, which is crucial for a healthy lipid profile.

> **Could Contribute To Maintaining Dental Health**

Stevia is a well-liked addition in toothpaste and mouthwash since it has been found to inhibit the growth of bacteria in the mouth. Unlike sucrose, which most likely doesn't do this, it may also help prevent cavities and gingivitis.

> **It Might Aid In Enhancing Skin Care**

Skin disorders, including eczema and dermatitis, can be treated with stevia. It is a common option for most people who can't find relief from these illnesses because its topical use prevents the spread of bacteria and functions as a steroid in these circumstances.

Side Effects

Food and Drug Administration (FDA) has designated the highly refined stevia types, like Truvia, as being unfit for human consumption. Although stevia in its leaf and extract forms is harmless, further research is required to fully understand its potential implications on human health. However, studies still support its use as a food additive and sweetener. Also, diabetes and low blood pressure patients should check their blood pressure and sugar levels, respectively, after consuming stevia. There have been instances of circumstances getting worse. Before including this in your diet, it is strongly advisable that you speak with your doctor, especially if you have any of those conditions.

Tips For Use

Stevia leaves, leaf powder, or liquid form can be used as a direct sugar substitute in a variety of meals, including:

- ✓ **Beverages:** For coffee and tea.
- ✓ **Dairy products:** For yogurt and ice cream.
- ✓ **Packed foods:** For pickles, sauces, soft drinks, and candy.
- ✓ **Baked goods:** For bread, cakes, and sweets.

You might even use it to prepare a variety of meals at home. It is significantly sweeter than sugar, thus it's crucial to measure the quantity before using it as a replacement.

How To Harvest Stevia

To create fresh tea or liquid extract, separate the leaves from the stems. Additionally, you can hang the stems and bundles of leaves in a cool, dark location until the leaves are completely dry. Harvest the entire plant in fall once temperatures have fallen.

36. St. John's Wort

A blooming plant known as St. John's wort (Hypericum perforatum) is called so for the vivid yellow blooms that are supposed to have opened after the first time around the feast day of St. John the Baptist. In Old English, "wort" is a term that means "plant." According to some of these researches, St. John's wort may be just as effective as over-the-counter antidepressants for treating mild depression as both a placebo and sugar tablet. St. John's wort was found in two American studies to be no more effective at treating moderate to severe depression than a placebo.

Health Benefits Of St. John's Wort

The health benefits of St. John's Wort are:

- A decrease in symptoms of depression
- A decline in signs of menopause
- Supports wound healing (when applied to the skin as a lotion)

Side Effects

Short-term oral St. John's wort supplement users may encounter negative consequences. These might include:

- Slight stomach discomfort
- Diarrhea
- Dry mouth
- Headache
- Tiredness
- Dizziness
- Anxiety
- Restlessness
- Tingling
- Skin allergies
- Either sexual or erectile dysfunction
- Vivid dreams
- Damage to the liver
- Psychosis (rare)

A skin rash could develop if St. John's wort is applied topically. The sensitivity of your skin and eyes to sunlight may also worsen if you use St. John's wort (topically or orally). St. John's wort has dangers and advantages that should be discussed with your doctor or pharmacist if you have a condition like lupus or are taking a medication that can make you photosensitive (like some medications for acne).

Tips For Use

Below are tips on how to use St. John's Wort:

- ✓ **Tea:** To make tea, add one teaspoon of herb to one cup of boiling water. Steep for five to ten minutes. Drink one to three times each day.
- ✓ **Tincture:** For a cup of hot water or lemon balm tea, mix two to three droppers of the tincture into the liq uid.
- ✓ **Capsules/Tablets:** Numerous studies have been conducted on goods that are guaranteed to contain particular concentrations of important substances. In the search for supplements that are standardized to 0.3 percent hypericin or 3 to 5 percent hyperforin, 900 to 1,500 mg per day is the recommended dosage for these products.

How To Harvest St. John's Wort

The optimal time to harvest and utilize St. John's wort is when it has fully bloomed and still fresh, but it is acceptable if part of the blooms have slightly dried out on the stem. It is ready for harvesting if you press the flower buds between your fingers and notice a red material, that is, hypericin, the primary medicinal component. Cut the plant's top 2-3 inches off to collect the leaves, flowers, and buds, as each has various benefits. Make sure to pick St. John's wort in an area free of sprays and road runoff because it freq uently grows in places that aren't good for foraging, in particular, roadsides.

37. Thyme

Thyme (Thymus vulgaris) is a hardy, shrubby herb with trailing, green-gray leaves with a potent flavor and perfume. This herb can also be found in drier, sunnier regions of Western Asia and southern Europe. It is indigenous to the western Mediterranean. It's also the variety that appears most freq uently in historical recipes and cures, particularly those from and related to ancient Greece, Rome, and Egypt. Thyme not only gives food an instant flavor boost, but it also has health advantages when eaten fresh, dried, or steeped in tea.

Health Benefits Of Thyme

Below are the health benefits of using thyme:

> ## Aids In The Battle Against Cancer

Thyme may aid in the prevention of cancer, especially colon cancer, according to research. These q ualities can be related to its ingredients, some of which include oleanolic acid, ursolic acid, lutein, and beta-sitosterol. Breast cancer can also be prevented using thyme. The herb has demonstrated beneficial effects in the treatment of breast cancer by perhaps boosting the death of cancer cells. A study discovered that carvacrol can suppress the growth and migration of cancer cell lines, making it another important component of thyme essential oil that prevents cancer. The substance has therapeutic effects on the management and potential prevention of cancer, particularly colon cancer.

> ## Increases Immunity

Thyme helps white blood cells to develop, thereby strengthening the immune system. Additionally, its anti-inflammatory actions aid in enhancing immunity. It can be used in a steam tent to relieve congestion and a cold because of its moderate flavor and fragrance. Thyme can hasten the healing of wounds. It can help with this by using its local application.

➢ Enhances Digestive Health

Thyme is well known for limiting the production of toxic gases in the stomach, improving digestion. The thyme's volatile oils, which have carminative (reducing gas) qualities, are responsible for this effect. Additionally, thyme acts as an antispasmodic and eases cramps in the intestines.

➢ Enhances Eye Health

Vitamin A, a substance particularly good for eye health, is abundant in thyme. A vitamin A shortage can cause night blindness. Thyme may also aid in preventing macular degeneration and other vision-related problems.

➢ Helps With Dyspraxia Treatment

Dyspraxia is a neurological condition that impairs movement and known as Developmental Coordination Disorder (DCD). It has been discovered that thyme helps with the symptoms of this illness, particularly in youngsters. In a study to determine the effectiveness of essential oils in the treatment of neurological conditions, like dyspraxia, thyme oil was one of the oils utilized. The study's findings also appeared promising.

Side Effects

Thyme is freq uently ingested in foods when taken orally. Short-term medical usage of thyme may be secure. Some individuals may experience allergic reactions, vertigo, and stomach distress. Thyme oil may be safe for short-term use when applied topically.

Skin irritation may occur in some people. There isn't enough trustworthy data to determine whether thyme oil is safe to use or what potential adverse effects there may be when it is inhaled.

Tips For Use

Below are tips on how to use thyme:

✓ **Tea:** Steep one to two teaspoons of thyme leaves and blossoms in a cup of hot water, then drink three times daily.

✓ **Syrups and capsules:** Thyme extracts come in a range of dosages and potencies as syrups and capsules. Thyme is frequently included in these medications along with other herbs that are supposed to help with respiratory issues; however, each product has a different intended application.

How To Harvest Thyme

When you are prepared to harvest from your thyme plants, you will need sterilized pruners or garden shears. Since you are opening a wound when you harvest thyme, using clean eq uipment can help keep your plants healthy. Your plants may become vulnerable to diseases or pest infestations if you pinch or rip off leaves or stems. When harvesting, take young, fresh sprigs or leaves. Avoid taking cuttings of the plants' woody portions. Although less fragrant and not the best for cooking, these woody parts are crucial for the plant to thrive. During fall, refrain from harvesting after the plants have set seed. Cooking will not be the best use of the flavors. You can take the blossoms out in summer to keep them from setting seed. Take no more than one-third of the plant at a time. Thyme benefits from periodic harvests of a single sprig or two. This type of gentle trimming will encourage development into a full and bushy shape. When harvesting, make sure to spread out your collections rather than only taking from one spot on the plant. Cut above a leaf node to promote bushier growth and increase the likelihood of future harvests!

38. Tumeric

Turmeric (Curcuma longa) is a spice that is made from the root of the Curcuma longa plant, a perennial member of the ginger family. Curcumin is the primary active component. Turmeric's yellow hue is caused by curcumin. The health advantages of curcumin are turmeric's greatest asset. Antioxidant and anti-inflammatory effects are found in curcumin.

Health Benefits Of Turmeric

The spice, which is simple to incorporate into smoothies and curries, shows promise in terms of the following health benefits.

> ### ➢ Reduces Inflammation

Taking turmeric may be helpful if you have a chronic illness where your body's tissues start to become affected by inflammation. In a study of people with ulcerative colitis, those who added two grams of curcumin to their daily dose of prescription medication had a higher chance of maintaining their remission than those who only took the medication.

> ### ➢ Reduces Pain

In both Ayurveda and Chinese traditional medicine, turmeric has a long history of use for treating arthritis. Taking turmeric extract, according to research, may help lessen osteoarthritis discomfort.

> **Neutralizes Free Radicals**

Due to its antioxidant characteristics, one study suggests that turmeric may shield your body from free radicals by scavenging them. Another survey contends that the antioxidant properties of turmeric may potentially promote the activity of additional antioxidants.

> **Reduces The Risk Of Heart Disease**

Turmeric may help lessen the risk of heart disease by reducing oxidation and inflammation. Resistance artery endothelial production, which significantly contributes to high blood pressure, was elevated in healthy middle-aged and older persons who took curcumin pills for twelve weeks. When combined with other medications for controlling cholesterol, turmeric may also be beneficial. Curcumin is safe, according to research, and it may help patients who are at risk of heart disease by lowering specific cholesterol levels.

> **Reduces Depression**

Your hippocampus, which aids in learning and memory, begins to shrink if you have depression, and brain-derived neurotrophic factor (BDNF) levels are decreased. Curcumin can raise BDNF levels and possibly counteract changes. According to a different study, the antidepressant properties of curcumin are comparable to those of fluoxetine (Prozac). Serotonin and dopamine are two substances in the brain that control mood and other bodily functions, may also be increased by curcumin.

Side Effects

Turmeric is probably safe for short-term use when taken orally. It appears that using turmeric products that contain up to 8 grams of curcumin per day for up to two months is safe. It also seems that eating up to 3 grams of turmeric per day for up to three months is safe. In most cases, turmeric doesn't have harmful side effects. Mild side effects, like nausea, diarrhea, dizziness, and upset stomach, are possible for some persons. Higher doses are more likely to cause these negative effects. Turmeric is probably safe when administered topically. Turmeric might be risk-free when used as a mouthwash. Turmeric may also be safe when used as an enema by applying it to the rectum.

Tips For Use

- ✓ **Tea:** Boil two cups of water, add one teaspoon of turmeric, and let simmer for ten minutes. If desired, incorporate honey or lemon.
- ✓ **Capsules:** Take 2 to 3 grams of turmeric per day because it offers 60 to 100 mg of curcumin, which is the usual daily intake in India's diet.
- ✓ **Extract:** To duplicate the curcumin concentrations used in clinical research on turmeric, get an extract that ensures a particular level of curcumin (sometimes written as curcuminoid on the label). In majority of investigations,

curcumin dosages of 1 to 2 g per day, divided into two to three doses, were utilized in turmeric extracts.

How To Harvest Turmeric

Use a garden fork or trowel to dig up the entire plant, being careful not to pierce the tubers, to collect turmeric. Shake off the soil and gently pick all the roots and tubers out of the ground. Once the fresh turmeric root has been picked, trim the fibrous roots and foliage before washing the tubers under cool running water.

39. Valerian

The herbal treatment known as valerian root (scientific name, Valeriana officinalis) has roots in ancient Greece. Pink or white blooms are found on valerian plants. Although it was once only found in Europe and Asia, it is now also found in North America. This medicinal plant can be found in a variety of forms, such as tinctures, tablets, and teas.

Health Benefits Of Valerian

Among valerian root's health benefits are:

> ### It Controls Anxiety And Stress

In order to cope with the stress brought on by air attacks, many in the UK consumed valerian root during World War II. It was used by medical professionals to treat the symptoms of anxiety before that, in the 1500s. Anxiolytic is a term used to describe an anti-anxiety property, and preliminary research suggests that valerian root may have this effect. However, more studies are req uired. Early research suggests that the anxiety-reducing component of valerian root may be valerenic acid. This early investigation found that this acid not only had anti-anxiety properties but also did not bind to the brain's benzodiazepine receptors. According to research, benzodiazepine addiction may be caused by these receptors. Pharmaceuticals of the benzodiazepine class are freq uently used for anxiety. While being less addictive than benzodiazepines, valerenic acid may help with anxiety.

➤ Reduced Hot Flashes In Menopausal Women

Research shows that valerian root supplementation reduced menopausal women's hot flashes by lowering their intensity and freq uency. Some people find hot flashes uncomfortable because they result in sweating, a quick heartbeat, and a sudden warmth. Hot flashes are brought on by hormonal changes. Those who want to lessen hot flashes can use hormonal therapy. For those who have a higher risk of heart disease, blood clots, stroke, or breast cancer, these therapies might not be appropriate. Taking valerian root supplements may be beneficial for those looking for alternative treatments.

➤ Decrease In Premenstrual Symptoms

Premenstrual syndrome (PMS) symptoms are experienced by 90% of menstruating individuals. When it comes to living a normal life around the time of their period, some people have PMS that is so severe that it interferes with it. PMS symptoms consist of:

- Bloating
- Irritability
- Cramps
- Headache
- Backache
- Painful and swollen breasts
- Lots of fatigue
- Anxiety
- Depression
- Mood swings
- Desire for food

One study found that valerian root supplementation may lessen the severity of PMS symptoms on both the physical and emotional levels.

Side Effects

Valerian is probably safe for short-term usage when taken orally. Up to six weeks of daily use of 300–600 mg of valerian has been proven to be safe. Long-term use's safety is uncertain. Generally, people tolerate valerian. Dizziness, drowsiness, headaches, stomach distress, mental dullness, and vivid dreams are some of the most typical adverse effects. Symptoms of withdrawal may appear if it is stopped after a prolonged use. After long-term use, it's preferable to gradually reduce the dose over a week or two before discontinuing altogether to prevent withdrawal symptoms.

Tips For Use

Below are tips on how you can use valerian root:

- ✓ **Tea:** To make a cup of tea, steep one teaspoon of dried valerian root in water for ten minutes. Drink something before going to sleep.
- ✓ **Capsule:** Take 2 to 3 g of dried valerian root each capsule, 30 to 60 minutes before bedtime.
- ✓ **Extract:** In clinical investigations, valerian extract doses standardized to valerenic acid ranging from 300 to 900 mg were utilized.
- ✓ **Tincture:** Usually 5 to 10 ml taken 30 to 60 minutes before bed.

How To Harvest Valerian Roots

Using a pair of garden shears, cut the stems off the plants close to the root. Accessing the roots is much simpler as a result. Use a shovel or garden fork to gently pull the roots from the soil of each plant you've decided to harvest. If the roots separate, you can carefully pull out the remaining roots with your hands. After shaking off the dirt, use your garden hose to thoroughly clean the roots. After rinsing the roots, you can bring them inside your kitchen and use a paper towel to pat them dry.

40. Witch Hazel

Witch hazel (Hamamelis virginiana) is a rare natural shrub that grows in eastern North America (range map).

It is a perennial bush that only reaches a height of a few meters and has numerous stems that develop from the roots. Witch hazel is a typical decorative plant that grows wild in moist lowlands and along streams and drainage ditches. Showy variants have been cultivated to resemble pompoms in appearance, and the distinctive blooms have the appearance of streamers bursting out of the central petal.

Health Benefits Of Witch Hazel

Witch hazel has the following health benefits:

➤ It Reduces Inflammation

An immune response called inflammation helps your body fight against infection and harm. The development of several diseases, however, is known to be heavily influenced by chronic inflammation. Numerous substances, notably tannins and gallic acid, found in witch hazel have strong anti-inflammatory effects. Additionally, it has antioxidants that fight against free radicals, substances that can accumulate in your body and cause diseases, and avoid extensive inflammation. Witch hazel may, therefore, have numerous advantages and be helpful in the treatment of such conditions as eczema, psoriasis, and acne that are inflammatory in nature.

➤ Reduces Skin Irritability

An estimated 45% of Americans are said to suffer from sensitive skin, a disorder characterized by unusual sensory complaints. According to some studies, applying witch hazel topically to sensitive skin may help treat it when irritated, inflamed, or damaged. It has been demonstrated that witch hazel reduces erythema, a skin reddening brought on by damage or irritation. An analogous small study discovered that a topical witch hazel treatment could soothe inflamed or sensitive face skin.

➤ Aids In Hemorrhoid Treatment

Hemorrhoids are characterized by symptoms, like itching and bleeding, brought on by the enlargement and inflammation of the veins in your rectum and anus.

Witch hazel is frequently used as a home treatment to ease the discomfort and agony associated with hemorrhoids. To calm the skin, it is often incorporated into a cloth or cotton ball and administered directly to the troubled area. Witch hazel is also thought to have anti-inflammatory properties that may help treat hemorrhoids' itchiness, redness, discomfort, and swelling. Additionally, it possesses hemostatic qualities, which means that it might reduce hemorrhoidal bleeding.

➤ Battles Acne

The best results come from using it immediately on your face after cleansing or steaming. Along with relaxing your skin and reducing inflammation, it works as an astringent, causing your tissues to tighten, aiding in reducing pores. By doing so, you might stop skin infections brought on by germs that cause acne. Witch hazel is frequently used in numerous over-the-counter acne products because of this, and it is especially beneficial for people with oily skin.

> **Reduces Sensitivity Of The Scalp**

Skin diseases, such as psoriasis or seborrheic dermatitis, as well as cosmetic hair treatments, can all contribute to scalp irritation. Before washing your hair, dab some witch hazel on your scalp to treat scalp sensitivity and ease symptoms, like itching and discomfort. Inflammation may also be reduced with witch hazel, which may be helpful in lowering scalp sensitivity brought on by psoriasis or eczema. In other cases, it's utilized as a home remedy to treat the signs of other scalp issues, such as dandruff and dryness.

Side Effects

Studies have shown that witch hazel rarely causes allergic responses. Healthcare professionals consider witch hazel safe when administered topically; however, it should not be ingested. Witch hazel consumption can result in issues, like nausea, vomiting, and liver damage. For those who have rosacea, a skin condition that makes your face red and causes swelling bumps to appear, witch hazel is not advised. Before using witch hazel, talk to your doctor if you have dry or sensitive skin.

Tips For Use

Below are tips on how to use witch hazel:

✓ **Extract:** The process of distilling the leaves, bark, and/or twigs yields many different types of witch hazel. This liq uid is made into creams or ointments before being administered to the skin.

✓ **Liquid:** Plant components are soaked in water to make witch hazel water, which is then distilled. To prevent the distillate from deteriorating, alcohol is added (for example, 86 percent witch hazel distillate and 14 percent alcohol). Generally speaking, tinctures and other herbal medicine-related preparations are stronger than distilled witch hazel water.

How To Harvest Witch Hazel

Remove the leaves and cut the twigs into somewhat little pieces, each about an inch long (2.5 cm). Using a little knife, you can remove the outer bark from bigger twigs or branches.

41. Chickweed

chickweed (Stellaria media), an annual plant that is native to Europe has naturalized in North America but is primarily regarded as a weed. However, chickweed is a strong and well-known human treatment said to provide considerable health advantages, according to herbalists and alternative medicine practitioners. It has been used for long to prepare oral decoctions, extracts, and teas, but chickweed's flowers, leaves, and stems are also employed. As a topical ointment, chickweed is becoming more freq uently utilized to treat a range of skin disorders. Despite being popular in some cultures, it is usually advised against eating chickweed due to the possibility of negative effects. The distinctive characteristics of chickweed include its hairy stalks, oval leaves, and small, daisy-like blooms with five crenelated petals.

Health Benefits Of Chickweed

Among chickweed's health benefits are:

> **Coughs/Colds/Flu**

Chickweed includes saponins, natural substances that can soothe inflamed mucus membranes and make it easier for membrane secretions to be broken up. It has demulcent and expectorant properties that assist remove mucus and reduce lung congestion. Chickweed, also rich in numerous nutrients, including vitamin C and antioxidants, helps reduce inflammation in the nose, sinuses, and respiratory system while also assisting in eradicating the underlying infection.

> **Optimal Weight Loss**

Chickweed's saponins have been discovered to emulsify fat cells and expel them from the body, acting as a natural appetite suppressant. The healthy thyroid function that is necessary for the efficient operation of the body's metabolism is supported by this adaptable herb as well. The natural lecithin included in it specifically helps with fat metabolism.

> **Digestive Wellness**

By enhancing mucus membrane's permeability and calming the digestive tract, the aforementioned saponins found in chickweed also promote nutritional absorption. Both as a moderate laxative and a diuretic, it aids the body in eliminating toxins through the kidneys and bowels. Chickweed's ability to balance the good bacteria in the stomach creates the ideal environment for optimal digestion.

> **Skin Wellness**

In the field of modern herbalism, chickweed is well known as a skin rejuvenator. It treats cuts, bites, and small burns by chilling and drying them off. Chickweed can be used as an astringent to remove splinters and aid in the healing of the wound left behind.

Infusions of chickweed can be used to treat a variety of skin conditions, such as boils, blisters, rashes, wounds, eczema, and psoriasis. They also have anti-inflammatory, antibacterial, and antifungal effects. It will help reduce inflammation and itchiness common with most of these diseases.

Side Effects

Large doses of the infusion have been associated with human episodes of paralysis.

Tips For Use

Consume 1-2 handfuls of chickweed each day, being sure to include the leaf, flower, and stem. To prepare tea, use one heaping tablespoon, and let it steep for ten to fifteen minutes for every cup of boiling water. Take 2 to 3 cups daily. For therapeutic effects, chickweed is often used for a few weeks to several months.

How To Harvest Chickweed

Cut the fragile new growth using scissors, or only remove the top couple of inches from more mature plants.

42. Lemongrass

Cymbopogon citratus, sometimes known as lemongrass, is a tall, stalky plant. It tastes citrusy and has a fresh, lemony scent. It is both a major component in Thai cooking and natural insect repellant. In aromatherapy, lemongrass essential oil is used to freshen the air, lower stress levels, and improve mood. Additionally, lemongrass is employed as a folk treatment to improve immunity, ease discomfort, and enhance sleeping. Tea is among the most common ways to consume lemongrass. Continue reading to find out how consuming lemongrass tea might contribute to these potential health advantages.

Health Benefits Of Lemongrass

The following are some of lemongrass' health benefits:

> **It Contains Anti-Oxidant Qualities**

Numerous antioxidants found in lemongrass can assist your body scavenge free radicals that could potentially lead to diseases. Chlorogenic acid and isoorientin are noteworthy antioxidants. These antioxidants can stop the cells inside your coronary arteries from malfunctioning.

➤ It Could Lower Your Risk Of Developing Cancer

Lemongrass is believed to have powerful anticancer properties against some cancer cell lines, thanks to its citral content. Lemongrass contains a number of anti-cancer ingredients. This happens either by directly killing cancer cells or strengthening your immune system so that your body can fight against cancer more effectively. When receiving chemotherapy or radiation, lemongrass tea is occasionally used as an adjuvant therapy. Only an oncologist's advice should be sought before using it.

➤ It Could Facilitate A Healthy Digestive System

If you have an upset stomach, stomach cramps, or any other digestive issues, try a cup of lemongrass tea as a substitute treatment. Lemongrass has been shown to have the potential to treat gastrointestinal ulcer, according to research. The study determined that the stomach lining can be shielded from harm by aspirin and ethanol with the help of lemongrass essential oil. Gastric ulcers are freq uently caused by regular aspirin use.

➤ It May Alleviate Insomnia

It's believed that drinking lemongrass tea can help relax the body and calm the mind, which may promote sleeping. Lemongrass tea has calming qualities, according to research, which may contribute to longer sleep cycles.

> ➤ **Potential Treatment For Respiratory Conditions**

Due to its therapeutic properties in the treatment of colds and coughs, lemongrass is freq uently employed in Ayurvedic medicine.

It has Vitamin C that, along other healthy ingredients, may aid in easing the symptoms offlu, bronchial asthma, and other respiratory conditions, like blocked noses.

Side Effects

When used in food, lemongrass is probably safe for most individuals. It is secure when ingested or topically used for a brief period for medical purposes. However, there have been some harmful side effects, such as lung issues, after inhaling lemongrass and deadly poisoning after a youngster ingested an insect repellant containing lemongrass oil.

Tips For Use

You'll enjoy utilizing your lemongrass almost as much as you do growing it. Here are some ideas on how you can use it:

✓ **Lemongrass tea:** This is the ideal approach to utilize the lemongrass plant's portions that lack sufficient flavors for cooking. A few sections of the fresh, dried, or outer woody stalks, cut into 1- or 2-inch lengths, should be steeped in a cup of boiling water for 5 minutes, or longer if you want a stronger coffee. Add sugar or honey to taste. Both hot and chilled lemongrass tea are delectable.

- ✓ **Ginger alternative:** Any dish flavor profile will be softer if lemongrass is used instead of ginger.
- ✓ **Topper or garnish for a salad:** For this use, mince the stalk's softer sections.
- ✓ **Alternative to lemon juice:** Cream sauces can substitute lemongrass for lemon juice without the risk of the sauce curdling.
- ✓ **Adding flavor to sauces, broths, and other dishes:** Any recipe that would benefit from a delicate, lemony flavor can be enhanced using lemongrass stalks or leaves. Use it like how you would utilize a bay leaf, and take it out just before serving.

How To Harvest Lemongrass

The stalk and foliage of lemongrass are both used in harvesting. You can start picking lemongrass as soon as the plant is about a foot tall. Offset a stalk that is at least 1/4 inch thick by cutting, twisting, or breaking. The bottom is the most delicate part, so cut it off as near to the ground as you can. Remove the woody outer layer and leaves once you've harvested the desired amount of stalks. Save the leaves and compost them after drying. Slice the stalk's soft portion, and add to your recipe as needed. You can freeze or refrigerate extra lemongrass.

43. Marjoram

An aromatic herb known as marjoram (Origanum majorana) is utilized for its citrus and pine tastes. Marjoram is a shrub native to the Middle East and Mediterranean region used to flavor a variety of foods. To distinguish it from oregano or "wild marjoram," marjoram can also be made into a herbal tisane and is frequently referred to as "sweet marjoram." Most supermarkets carry dried marjoram in the spice section; health food and specialized shops carry fresh leaves, oil extracts, and tea bags.

Health Benefits Of Majoram

Marjoram can have significant health benefits and has been utilized in many conventional and folk medicines. For instance, it has been demonstrated that substances produced from marjoram have anti-inflammatory, antibacterial, and antioxidant properties. Marjoram also has other health benefits, such as:

➢ **Hormone Balance**

Marjoram may be helpful for women's hormonal health. According to research, women with PCOS who drink marjoram tea twice daily for a month can enhance their insulin sensitivity and lower their levels of adrenal androgens.

> ## Relief From Anxiety

Marjoram has been found to have anxiolytic or anxiety-reducing effects. Marjoram oil aromatherapy improves the anxiety-relieving effects of neurofeedback training in patients who grind their teeth.

> ## Antimicrobial Activity

The antibacterial properties of marjoram have been demonstrated in numerous investigations. One study discovered that marjoram essential oil works well against a variety of pathogenic microorganisms. Another found marjoram oil to be an efficient complementary treatment for urinary tract infections (UTIs) brought on by E. coli bacteria.

Side Effects

Marjoram is likely safe when taken orally in food. For the majority of individuals, it is secure when used as medicine in higher doses for brief periods of time. Long-term usage of marjoram is dangerous. Some worry that long-term usage of marjoram may have negative effects on the kidneys, liver, and even cause cancer. Also, some individuals have allergies to marjoram when applied to the skin.

Tips For Use

Why not try making tea with marjoram if you're looking for a way to use it? Making this herbal tea is simple and a great way to experience the flavor of the herb. To prepare Marjoram tea, you will need:

- ✓ One teaspoon marjoram, fresh or dried
- ✓ Eight ounces of boiling water
- ✓ Honey (optional)

Process:

Just combine the marjoram with a cup of boiling water to make the tea, and let it steep for five minutes. To sweeten the tea, if you'd like, you can add a little honey. Strain the tea after it has finished steeping, then savor it!

How To Harvest Marjoram

Harvest marjoram leaves during summer as needed by first snipping off a few shots, then removing the leaves. Before the flower buds bloom, the flavor is at its peak. Use the fresh or dried leaves. Ice-cube trays can also be used to freeze them.

44. Sweet Violet

Sweet violet (Viola odorata) is a herb. Medicine is made from the root and components that grow above the ground. In addition to many other illnesses, sweet violet is used to treat stress, exhaustion, sleeplessness, menopause symptoms, depression, common cold, and influenza. You will learn more about the benefits as we go on.

Health Benefits of Sweet Violet Leaves

We might presume that sweet violet leaves have a number of health benefits for our bodies based on their nutritional worth. Thus, consistent use and intake of sweet violet leaves can provide the following health benefits:

➤ Decreasing Blood Pressure

Due to the presence of alkaloids and flavonoids, the leaves of the violet plant can lower blood pressure. Blood vessels can relax, thanks to alkaloids. Our blood flow will be improved as a result. Having a healthy blood circulation, as we all know, keeps our blood pressure from rising. The diuretic properties of flavonoids, on the other hand, make them advantageous for people with high blood pressure. Accordingly, high blood pressure is successfully decreased. Since regular blood pressure will keep our hearts healthy, we may, thus, conclude that these heart-shaped leaves are beneficial to our hearts.

➤ Cancer Treatment

According to research, violet leaves can help prevent and treat cancer in its early stages. The ability to combat free radicals, which are the primary cause of cancer growth, is a result of the high antioxidant levels. It goes without saying that regular ingestion of violet leaves can lessen or decrease cancerous tumors in their early stages.

➤ Improve Digestion

The soluble fiber or mucin in violet leaves helps lower levels of harmful cholesterol. Additionally, it is beneficial for enhancing gut flora health.

Intestinal flora provides the beneficial microorganisms that facilitate digestion with food. Additionally, dietary fiber can help with bowel movements and issues with digestion, like gas and constipation.

> ### Minimize Inflammation

Usually, wild plants are grown. But you ought to be aware that this plant is actually valuable. The flower can be admired for its exquisiteness and uniq ue hue. In addition, we can use both flowers and leaves for our food needs. You can get nourishment from it as well as the health advantages of violet leaves. Reduced inflammation is one of the health advantages of violet leaves. The anti-inflammatory properties of leaves are strong. It can reduce various forms of inflammation, including sinusitis, bronchitis, and sore throats.

> ### Relief Cough

Violet leaves may help you stop coughing if it's uncontrollable. Due to the presence of substances that are good for the lungs, like mucilage and saponins, violet decoction or hot violet tea can be a potent expectorant. It is also recommended as a bronchitis treatment.

> ### Purifies The Blood

Blood can be purified using the leaves of lovely violet flowers. It implies that the leaves are advantageous for enhancing metabolism. Additionally, leaves speed up the removal of waste. Consuming violet leaves stimulates the lymphatic glands, which aid in clearing the blood of bacteria and other unwanted substances.

Side Effects

When taken orally, sweet violet is probably safe in the dosages seen in meals. When administered as nose drops, sweet violet is generally safe for use for up to 30 days. When used topically, sweet violet oil is secure when utilized as directed.

Tips For Use

- ✓ **Infusion:** To make an infusion, prepare the leaves and blossoms as directed, let them steep for at least four hours, then serve.
- ✓ **Tincture:** For adults, use 30 to 40 drops of the tincture Viola tricolor two to five times each day.
- ✓ **Syrup:** For insomnia, use one to five teaspoons of violet flower syrup daily.
- ✓ **Topical preparations:** This should be made as a wash, poultice, or oil and applied as needed, increasing the frequency with the severity of the problem.

How To Harvest Sweet Violet

Violets should first be washed and allowed to wilt. Overnight exposure to the elements will help the violets lose some of their moisture. You can choose to use the complete flower or, if you wish, you can remove all the petals, which results in a more uniform violet color.

45. Stinging Nettle

Since ancient times, stinging nettle (Urtica dioica) has been a mainstay in herbal therapy. Stinging nettle was used as a remedy for arthritis and lower back discomfort by the ancient Egyptians, while Roman soldiers applied it on their bodies to stay warm. Its scientific name, Urtica dioica, is derived from the Latin word uro, which means "to burn," because coming into contact with its leaves might temporarily make one feel burned. The leaves have stinging, irritating, reddening, and swelling hair-like features. Stinging nettle can, however, be eaten without any risk after being turned into a supplement, dried, freeze-dried, or cooked.

Health Benefits Of Stinging Nettle

Here are some benefits of stinging nettle supported by research:

> ## Maintains Healthy Levels Of Blood Pressure And Sugar

Stinging nettle is good at stabilizing blood sugar and pressure levels by lowering them. The risk of cardiovascular conditions, like heart attack and stroke, can be decreased by stinging nettle. Stinging nettle leaf extract, according to research, decreases type-2 diabetics' blood glucose levels.

> ## Helpful In Preventing A Variety Of Illnesses

According to research, nettle tea contains polyphenols, a plant component that aids in the management and prevention of chronic illnesses, like diabetes, cancer, heart disease, and obesity. Nettle tea also has anti-inflammatory qualities that could aid in regulating digestion and lowering diarrhea and constipation occurrences.

➢ Relieves Pain

Nettle tea's anti-inflammatory effects may help lessen the signs and symptoms of pain. Nettle tea can assist relieve discomfort from headaches, joint pain, and muscle pain.

➢ Soothes Skin Rashes And Allergies

Nettle tea has many advantages, from lowering skin irritation to easing allergic symptoms, even if the leaves can occasionally be itchy for the skin. Skin conditions, including eczema and acne, can be effectively treated with stinging nettle's antihistamines, anti-inflammatory, and antibacterial q ualities.

➢ Maintains The Health Of The Prostate, Kidney, And Urethra

In addition to kidney and prostate problems, nettle tea is used to treat UTIs.

Given its diuretic properties, nettle can both encourage regular urination and prevent the germs that lead to kidney stones and UTIs from growing. In addition to preventing kidney stones, nettle tea helps lessen the formation of calcium oxalate crystals in the kidneys.

Side Effects

Stinging nettle may be safe to use for up to a year when taken orally. Some people may experience diarrhea, constipation, and stomach discomfort as a result. It is possibly harmless when applied to the skin. Skin irritation can result from touching the stinging nettle plant.

Tips For Use

Depending on how it's used, different methods are employed to prepare stinging nettle. The Arthritis Foundation, for instance, advises consuming up to 1,300 mg of stinging nettle in the form of tea, capsules, tablets, tinctures, or extracts. As an alternative, consumers can take a tincture containing 1-4 mg daily or apply lotions directly to their skin. The Food and Drug Administration (FDA) doesn't control the components, potencies, or marketing claims of herbal treatments or dietary supplements. Stinging nettle goods are included in this. Therefore, it is advised that people utilize such items with prudence.

How To Harvest Stinging Nettle

Nettles can be harvested by removing only the upper leaves, which should be no wider than about three inches. Make sure there is no white spittle by inspecting the undersides of the leaves. Cutting the leaves off the stems as you go will save you a lot of time as you only need the leaves.

46. Borage

The plant known as borage (Borago officinalis) has long been recognized for its capacity to improve human health. Gamma linoleic acid (GLA), an omega-6 fatty acid that has been demonstrated to reduce inflammation, is particularly abundant in borege. Atopic dermatitis, rheumatoid arthritis, and asthma are just a few of the ailments that borage may aid in treating.

Borage, also referred to as starflower, is a herb renowned for its therapeutic benefits and vivid purple blossoms. The plant's leaves and blooms can be eaten, and are freq uently added as a garnish, dried herb, or vegetable to a variety of beverages and foods.

Health Benefits Of Borage

These are some health benefits of borage:

> ### Eliminates Inflammation

This particular benefit of borage seed oil must be attributed to gamma-linolenic acid. Your body transforms GLA, a crucial omega-6 fatty acid, into prostaglandins, which control inflammation and your immune system. Additionally, GLA exerts direct control on inflammatory cells, reducing inflammation. Additionally, the GLA in the oil contains anti-mutagenic q ualities and may possibly aid in the battle against cancer.

> ### Promotes Weight Loss

GLA, a crucial fatty acid, frequently results in a general improvement in health, which includes healthy weight loss. Additionally, GLA slows down the absorption of carbohydrates and helps your body hang onto proteins. The fat-soluble vitamins are also delivered to the bloodstream by the acid. Additionally, because GLA is a healthy fat, it reduces cravings for fat and prevents overeating. GLA simply prevents the body from storing as much fat. Even more intriguing, GLA reduces white fat while increasing brown fat growth. Brown fat is more common among leaner persons, according to research, and acts more like a muscle.

➤ Helps Treat Disorders Related To Acne

The GLA in borage seed oil aids in the reduction of inflammation, which might be crucial in the management of acne. Herbalists freq uently advice using the oil topically or internally for this purpose. The oil's anti-inflammatory q ualities aid in the treatment of diseases, like rosacea. The oil also lessens the condition related to skin reddening.

According to some sources, keratosis pilaris, another skin ailment that results in rough patches and bumps that resemble acne, can also be treated with borage oil.

➤ Enhanced Skin Health

Borage oil enhances the general health of the skin in addition to treating conditions, like acne and others. It treats dry skin and replenishes hydration. In particular, borage seed oil has the ability to cure dermatitis and eczema. This is explained by its capacity to make up for lipid deficits in the skin. According to science, inflammation and skin flare-ups occur when the skin cannot create enough of the protective oils.

Additionally, the oil can aid with psoriasis. Simply apply some borage oil to the troubled regions and let it sit there all night. Early in the morning, wash off with cold water.

➤ Treating Respiratory Allergies

Borage seed oil can enhance lung function, especially in people with inflammatory respiratory conditions, like Acute Respiratory Distress Syndrome (ARDS). Coughs, colds, and flu can all be treated with the oil. Additionally, bronchitis is frequently treated with it. Additionally, several research have shown that borage oil can be effective in treating other allergies. This also applies to asthma.

Side Effects

When properly ingested or applied to the skin, borage seed oil is harmless. When pyrrolizidine alkaloids (PAs), which are hazardous compounds, are present in goods containing borage seed oil, they pose a risk to human health. PAs can be found in the leaf, flower, and seed of the borage plant. Particularly when used in large doses or for an extended period, PAs might harm the liver or cause cancer.

Tips For Use

Borage seed oil clinical trials have employed doses of 1 to 3 g/day (up to 3 g/day for adults and 1 g/day for youngsters). Between 20 and 26% of the oil is gamma-linolenic acid (GLA), which is present in small amounts.

The dosage has been recommended as 2 g of dried herb steeped in a cup of hot water, taken three times daily. Adults with atopic dermatitis have been tested at oral dosages of 2,000–4,000 mg/day (GLA 400–1,000 mg), while children with the condition have been studied at oral doses of 1,000–2,000 mg/day (GLA 240–480 mg).

How To Harvest Borage

Borage is a plant whose edible leaves and blooms have a flavor reminiscent of cucumber. Fine, silvery hairs that are prone to becoming prickly as they age cover the stalks and leaves. Small amounts of silica, which might irritate certain people, are present in borage leaves. It is advisable to use gloves when selecting borage leaves and even in the kitchen if you are aware of or suspect you may be susceptible. Choose the young borage leaves while plucking them because they will include fewer fine hairs. Continuous harvesting and deadheading will extend the useful life.

47. Dandelion

Yellow blooms can be found on the dandelion plant (Taraxacum officinale). The most prevalent type of this plant, Taraxacum officinale, is found across the world. Botanists have classified dandelions as herbs. Dandelion roots, flowers, stems, and leaves are all medicinally used.

Health Benefits Of Dandelion

These are the health benefits:

> **Provide Antioxidants**

The roots, leaves, and flowers of dandelions all contain various kinds of antioxidants. Antioxidants shield the body from free radicals, errant chemicals that can harm your body's cells and hasten aging.

➤ Lessen Inflammation

A vast variety of significant health issues, including cancer and heart disease, are influenced by chronic inflammation in the body. Eating foods that fight inflammation is one approach to stay healthy. Include dandelion in your anti-inflammatory diet. According to research, these plants have substances that might reduce inflammation.

➤ Control Blood Pressure

Dandelions are a natural diuretic since they are high in potassium. In other words, they induce urination. Diuretics are freq uently used to lower blood pressure.

➤ Regulate Blood Sugar

The dandelion has been utilized to treat diabetes naturally all over the world. Studies on animals indicate that the chemicals in dandelions may help diabetics lower their blood sugar levels, but researchers are still looking into this connection.

➤ Reduce Cholesterol

The risk of heart disease can be significantly decreased by lowering cholesterol. Animal studies have shown that dandelion root and leaf extracts can naturally decrease cholesterol levels.

Side Effects

When consumed orally in proportions typically found in meals, dandelion is safe for the majority of people. When used orally in prescribed dosages, it is safe (larger amounts than those found in food). Dandelion consumption by mouth may result in heartburn, stomach pain, diarrhea, or allergic reactions in some persons.

Tips For Use

Dandelion leaves, stems, and flowers are freq uently eaten fresh or cooked in their natural state. Typically, the root is dried, ground, and used as an alternative to tea or coffee. Dandelion is sometimes offered as a dietary supplement in the form of capsules, extracts, or tinctures. Because there has been only a few human studies, there are currently no definitive dosage recommendations. However, the information at hand points to the following dosages for various dandelion forms:

- ✓ **Fresh leaves:** 4 to 10 grams daily
- ✓ **Dried leaves**: 4 to 10 grams daily
- ✓ **Leaf tincture:** 0.4–1 teaspoon (2–5 mL) of leaf tincture, three times daily.
- ✓ **Fresh leaf juice:** 1 teaspoon (5 mL), twice daily
- ✓ **Fluid extract:** 1 to 2 teaspoons (5 to 10 mL) each day
- ✓ **Fresh roots:** 2 to 8 grams daily
- ✓ **Dried powder:** take 250–1,000 mg four times daily.

How To Harvest Dandelion

Try to collect the little leaves of the plant before it blooms if you want to eat the dandelions. Taste the dandelion greens first to evaluate if the flavor is too repulsive once the yellow flower has opened. Pick off the tiny leaves to harvest, then consume right away.

48. Raspberry

The little, sweet fruit known as a raspberry (Rubus idaeus) has a tangy undertone. They may add a bright splash of color and delectable flavor to any bland meal to make it seem uniq ue. Additionally, every sweet raspberry is brimming with fiber, antioxidants, vitamins, and minerals. Red, black, purple, and gold are the four colors that raspberries come in. The most prevalent variety of raspberries at supermarkets is red. While frozen raspberries are readily available all year long and have the same nutritional value as fresh raspberries, fresh raspberries are often only available from June through October.

Health Benefits Of Raspberries

Raspberries provide the following health benefits:

➢ Helpful For Diabetics

Raspberries, especially red ones, are among the berries with the least sugar. For those who want to reduce their sugar intake while still satisfying their sweet tooth, this makes them a great option. Additionally, they have a glycemic index that is q uite low, which can aid in controlling blood sugar levels. Additionally, raspberries' high fiber contenthinders rapid digestion and aids in lowering blood sugar levels.

➢ Rich In Antioxidants

Antioxidants can be found in abundance in raspberries. They contain such elements as zeaxanthin, lutein, lycopene, and beta carotene. Antioxidants, according to studies, aid in reducing inflammation and preventing early aging. Very high free radical levels can harm our bodies' cells. Antioxidants also aid in the body's removal of free radicals, leading to several positive effects on health.

➢ Rich In Fiber

Red raspberries can have up to 8 g of dietary fiber in one cup. You will feel satisfied after consuming this fiber, which lessens the need to overeat. By delaying digestion, dietary fiber also delays blood sugar release. Additionally, it supports a healthy gut. Red raspberries aid in the formation of beneficial intestinal flora. Gut bacteria help in the development of immunity, a healthy digestive system, and improved food absorption. Moreover, evidence suggests that gut bacteria lower the risk of developing diseases.

> ## Good For The Heart

Various studies have determined that certain flavonoids found in red raspberries can help inhibit inflammation, which can result in cardiovascular diseases.

These flavonoids can reduce the immune response's severity. Additionally, antioxidants, like vitamin C, vitamin A, and many others, shield the cardiovascular system from possible damage brought on by free radicals. Furthermore, they contain potassium, which lowers blood pressure, raises blood circulation, and regulates sodium levels. As a result, it aids in lowering blood pressure.

> ## Regulates Cholesterol

Vitamin C and dietary fiber are abundant in raspberries. These vitamins and minerals can lower the harmful cholesterol. It also lessens the chance of atherosclerosis. In this disorder, plaque buildup causes the arteries to stiffen and narrow. Fiber stops this by regulating the body's creation of cholesterol. In addition to lowering LDL, the manganese in raspberries also helps regulate cholesterol and lowers the risk of cardiovascular diseases.

> ### Helpful Throughout Pregnancy

Numerous important vitamins, minerals, antioxidants, and fiber can be found in abundance in red raspberries. These substances are very important for keeping a pregnancy healthy. For instance, the vitamin C in red raspberries can aid in shielding the fetus from the harm caused by free radicals. They also have some folate in them. Studies have shown how important folate is for a fetus' healthy brain development. Numerous congenital defects may be less likely as a result. Besides, they are abundant in iron, zinc, and potassium, which are vital minerals for moms to keep their health during pregnancy.

Potential Side Effects

People who are allergic to salicylates can develop a raspberry allergy. You might have signs like:

- Tingling and itching in the mouth
- Swollen lips
- Runny nose
- Watery eyes
- Hives and sneezing
- Breathing problems

Tips For Use

Take roughly one teaspoon of crushed or dried raspberry leaves and put them into a cup before brewing a cup of red raspberry leaf tea. Once the cup is filled with hot water, allow it to steep for at least five minutes. You can then sip the tea. As an alternative, customers can follow the directions on the tea's label or purchase red raspberry leaf tea bags, which they can steep in boiling water for five minutes before drinking.

How To Harvest Raspberry

Grab the berry but don't squeeze it; just give it a light tug to harvest. The fruit is ripe if it easily separates from the stem and the core is still attached to the plant. Avoid collecting all the picked fruits in one container if there are numerous ripe berries at once; otherwise, you run the danger of having sq uashed berries.

49. Bay

Due to its delicate, herbal flavor, bay leaf (Laurus nobilis) is a spice that is freq uently used to season soups and meat preparations.

Although it is frequently discovered as a dry, entire leaf, it is occasionally offered in stores as powder or fresh leaves. Since the bay leaf is difficult to chew and digest alone, it is added during cooking and removed before a meal is served. Despite widespread belief, the bay leaf is not harmful.

Health Benefits Of Bay

When it comes to health advantages, a simple bay leaf may be q uite potent. Bay leaf boosts a dish's fiber, vitamin, mineral, and antioxidant content while only contributing a little amount of calories. Some of the bay's major health benefits are:

➢ **Immune System Health**

Vitamins A, B6, and C are abundant in bay leaf. All these vitamins have a reputation for supporting a robust immune system.

> ➤ **Digestive Assistance**

Bay leaf tea can help when you have stomach trouble. The tea also has a strong scent, which can help reduce nasal pressure or stuffiness.

> ➤ **Prevents Fungus Infestations**

The antifungal properties of bay leaf have been found to be effective against fungi. Along with its vitamin C concentration, these qualities can shield the skin from irritation and infection.

> ➤ **Reduces Tension And Anxiety**

Are you freq uently anxious? If yes, you should know that the linalool found in bay leaves can reduce the body's tension and anxiety level. Additionally, it has naturally calming properties that can aid in your calmness and lower the risk of depression.

> ➤ **Reduces The Risk Factors For Type 2 Diabetes**

According to one study, ingesting 1 to 2 grams of bay leaf daily for 30 days helps lower the chance of developing type 2 diabetes and heart disease. However, since the study on the effects of bay leaves on diabetes is still in its early stages, speak with your doctor before starting to use bay leaves to manage diabetes.

Side Effects of Bay Leaves

Bay leaf and bay leaf oil in dietary levels are probably harmless for most people. The complete, intact leaf should not be consumed.

Because the leaf cannot be digested, it stays whole as it moves through the digestive tract. This implies that it has the potential to obstruct the neck or puncture the intestines. Bay leaf may affect the regulation of blood sugar. Therefore, if someone has diabetes and uses a bay leaf as medicine, they need to constantly monitor their blood sugar. The central nervous system might be slowed by bay leaf (CNS). When used in conjunction with anesthetic and other drugs taken before, during, and after surgery, there is a concern that it may cause the CNS to slow down excessively. At least two weeks prior to the surgery, one should stop taking bay leaves as medicine.

Tips For Use

You can use bay leaves to make tea. The steps are given below:

To make tea, gather two large bay leaves, two cups of water, sugar, and milk (not required). Pour water into a pot and then cautiously add the bay leaf. At least three minutes of boiling should be allowed on high heat. Take the tea out of the saucepan and let it steep for a short period —say four minutes—before straining and drinking it. Sugar and milk are optional additions, but watch out—adding too much will change the tea's flavor.

How To Harvest Bay Leaves

When harvesting bay leaves, pick the biggest ones. A bay leaf has a stronger flavor as it ages, in contrast to other herbs that are at their best when young and fragile. As previously noted, bay leaves can be picked throughout the growing season, but if you want to harvest a large quantity at once, harvest around the middle of summer when the leaves are at their flavor and essential oil peak. Simply collect large, spotless bay leaves by hand-picking or with a knife. Spread the leaves out on a baking sheet lined with paper towels. Alternately, spread out each leaf separately, without touching, and let it dry on a piece of mesh screen.

50. Comfrey

Comfrey (Symphytum officinale) is a perennial shrub of European and partly Asian origin. Comfrey prefers moist soil and grows two to five feet tall with a thick, hairy stem. It has closely packed clusters of drab purple, blue, or pale blooms. The oblong leaves can vary in appearance depending on where they are located on the stalk.

Upper leaves are broad all the way through and only narrow at the ends, whereas lower leaves are broad at the base and taper at the ends. The root is black on the outside and white, meaty, and juice-filled inside. Comfrey preparations are created from the plant's leaves or other portions growing above the ground. In comparison to older leaves, new leaves typically contain more toxic pyrrolizidine alkaloids. Some preparations were also produced from the roots. However, the amount of pyrrolizidine alkaloids in the roots is up to 16 times higher.

Health Benefits Of Comfrey

Below are the health benefits of comfrey:

> **Enhanced Skin Health**

Comfrey-based creams and ointments are freq uently applied to sooth and treat sore or damaged nipples. Allantoin (0.6–4.7%) and rosmarinic acid (up to 0.2%) are both present in its roots. Allantoin protects and keeps the skin smooth. It aids in wound healing by encouraging the fibroblasts to make collagen. Comfrey's aerial components, such as its flowers and leaves, also have the ability to cure wounds. They may aid in the treatment of injuries and harsh traumas by promoting skin cell renewal. Anti-inflammatory qualities of allantoin lessen skin irritation and soothe an irritated skin. It keeps the skin hydrated and lessens aging symptoms to keep your skin looking young.

➢ Reduces Back Pain

Comfrey root extract applied topically can ease upper and lower back discomfort. Applying comfrey lotion three times per day was found to be helpful in the treatment of acute back pain in a trial involving 120 individuals. Faster relief is provided by comfrey root ointment, which can also lessen myalgia (soreness and muscle ache).

➢ Strengthens An Ankle Sprain

Ankle sprain symptoms can be lessened temporarily and the healing process sped up by using comfrey root ointment's medicinal capabilities.

For the treatment of ankle sprains, comfrey cream is superior than nonsteroidal anti-inflammatory medications. Furthermore, a scientific investigation revealed that plant-based ointments, such as comfrey ointment, are both safer and more potent than Diclofenac gel.

> ## Symptoms Of Osteoarthritis Are Lessened

In the United States, there are around 27 million persons who have osteoarthritis, a type of degenerative joint disease. Comfrey extract applied topically has been shown to effectively manage pain and increase knee mobility. Another option is to use lotions that combine tannic acid and extract from comfrey root. The stiffness and knee discomfort related to osteoarthritis can be relieved by taking this mixture three times daily for six weeks.

Side Effects Of Comfrey

Comfrey includes pyrrolizidine alkaloids, which are harmful substances that can harm the liver and perhaps kill you. FDA has outlawed oral comfrey products because of this. Comfrey topical preparations should not be used for an extended period because there is a possibility that it may absorb through the skin. Additionally, avoid using comfrey cream on open wounds. If you are breastfeeding, avoid using topical comfrey because it could expose the child to hazardous substances. Therefore, never self-medicate and always use comfrey lotions and ointments under a doctor's supervision.

Tips For Use

Comfrey, which is offered in creams, ointments, gels, and salve form, does not have a daily suggested dosage. Research has made use of the following applications:

- ✓ **Back Ache:** A topical medication comprising 1.2% methyl nicotinate and 35% comfrey root extract. Three times daily application for five days.
- ✓ **Osteoarthritis:** A particular topical cream that contains tannic acid, aloe vera gel, eucalyptus oil, and frankincense oil, as well as 35% comfrey root extract, may or may not. Three times a day for three to six weeks applied to the knee.
- ✓ **For Sprains:** Cream with 35% extract of comfrey. Four times every day for eight days applied to the ankle sprains.

How To Harvest Comfrey

The plant can be harvested q uite easily and simply. Cut the leaves back to a height of about two inches above the ground to begin. Additionally, you can take individual leaves as soon as they reach the size of your hand. You might anticipate a subsequent cutting after the initial one every six weeks until early October. Allowing the plants to leaf out at this time will help them prepare for winter.

CHAPTER FOUR: PRESERVING YOUR HERBS

Having a herb garden ensures that you always have the best, freshest herbs available for cooking endeavors. In other cases, it also means having too many herbs to utilize at once, which is a nice problem to have. We are all aware that herbs can be dried to be used later, but what about the herbs that are best utilized fresh? Can fresh herbs be preserved without being dried? Yes! For a detailed explanation on how to preserve fresh herbs, keep reading.

How To Preserve Fresh Herbs

Herbs can be preserved in a variety of methods:

1. Short-Term

Treating your herbs like cut flowers, cutting the stems at an angle with a sharp knife, and placing them right away in a container of fresh water, is the greatest way to extend the usage of your herbs for short runs of about a week. This technique is perfect for grocery store herbs that you want to keep fresh for a few days or longer. Herbs can be kept fresh for up to two weeks if the water is changed daily and the bouquet stored in the refrigerator.

2. Herbs Freezing

Fresh herbs can be frozen in their natural state by simply spreading them out in a layer on a baking sheet covered with parchment paper and freezing them. To accomplish this, wash and dry the herbs, then spread them out on a baking sheet covered with parchment paper. Finally, place the baking sheet with the herbs inside and freeze. Put them in a freezer bag or jar when they have frozen for later use. Rosemary and thyme are two herbs that have woody stems that are completely frozen naked. To separate the leaves from the stems, place the frozen sprigs in a bag and shake. Once the stems have been removed, gather the leaves and store them in a jar. When chopped, frozen, and then stored, chives and lemongrass are also perfectly frozen. After being briefly chilled, the leaves will not stick together.

3. Constructing A Herbal "Cigar"

It is difficult to freeze naked many fragile, broad-leaved herbs. Making them into a "cigar" is the best techniq ue to freeze certain types of herbs. With the stems cut off, separate the leaves, and place them in a freezer bag. Press the leaves firmly into the bottom of the bag, then roll it tightly to expel all the air until you reach the top, where you can seal it. Put the plastic bag in the freezer while retaining its rolled-up shape with elastic bands. When you're ready to use the herbs, take the rubber bands off, open the bag, and cut off only the amount of the "cigar" that you need before re-freezing. This method, which req uires less freezer space than freezing loose leaves, works well with cilantro, chervil, parsley, sage, tarragon, and other flat-leaved herbs.

4. Freezing In Ice Cubes

Some very delicate herbs that are best utilized fresh can be frozen in ice cube form. Herbs, like mint, cilantro, lemon balm, and others, can be preserved in this method to be used in recipes later. Simply put chopped or entire leaves into the individual cubes of an ice cube tray, fill halfway with water, and freeze for about an hour. Don't be concerned that the herbs will have risen to the top. Fill the tray to the top with them when they have frozen, then do it again. The herbs' color and flavor will be preserved by keeping them totally enclosed in ice, preventing oxidation. The frozen herb ice cubes can be moved from the tray into freezer bags or another sealed container for single-serving use whenever you need them. Cubes can be thrown straight into sauces or soups without needing to thaw beforehand. Additionally, ice cubes with herbs can be used in cocktails, like a mojito.

5. Frozen "Pesto" Cubes

Despite the fact that basil is often the first ingredient that comes to mind, not all pesto is created with it. When frozen bare, many herbs, including basil, oregano, marjoram, and others, become unsightly and dark. Frozen in a paste and suspended in oil, these herbs will remain at their most aesthetically pleasing and tasty.

To make this task as simple as possible, separate the leaves from the stems and add a cup of fresh herbs and 1/4 cup of olive oil to a food processor or blender. Pulse the ingredients until they are well-combined. When the mixture has frozen, move it to an airtight container for long-term storage before pouring it into ice cube trays. You can also do this with whole leaves; all you have to do is press them into ice cube trays, coat them with oil, and freeze.

6. Herbeb Butter

A simple DIY method for preserving fresh herbs so they're ready for stuffing, sautéing, or spreading is to make herbed butter. Although it's simple to create, herb butter has a rich feel. Use either salted or unsalted butter to preserve herbs in butter; the choice is entirely yours. After thoroughly drying the herbs, separate the leaves from the stems. Start by rinsing the herbs. Keep the butter at room temperature so that it can soften while the herbs are drying. Finely mince the herbs and, if preferred, season with salt or lemon zest. Mash the butter and herbs in a bowl until the mixture is consistent. Spread all the butter across a square of parchment paper that has been cut to size with a spatula. To form a log, roll the paper around the mixture. Put them in the fridge after folding the ends. Voila! Now you have butter with herbs. This is a great way to give your dish a little flair, and you can make blends that are appropriate for different cuisines. With the addition of lemon zest, parsley butter brightens up vegetables; basil butter goes well with fish or scrambled eggs; sage butter goes well with chicken or biscuits; and many combinations of herbs can be used in cooking. Almost any herb can be made into butter using a compound. It can be frozen, but it will remain in the fridge for a few weeks. Although it can be stored for six months, frozen herb butter is best used within two months. Beyond that, the q uality will deteriorate.

7. Herbed Salt

For devoted cooks, salting herbs is a highly pleasurable method to keep the season alive and add rich flavor to savory recipes. The addition of garlic results in a perfectly balanced spice blend that may be dry preserved without using a dehydrator or other specialized eq uipment.

Start with a half-cup of kosher salt, two cups of strong, fresh herbs—rosemary, thyme, savory, and sage are excellent choices—and four to five peeled garlic cloves. Mince the garlic and two teaspoons of salt in a food processor or with a chef's knife. The herbs should be chopped in a food processor or on a cutting board until the mixture resembles coarse sand. Sprinkle the remaining salt on top of the mixture after spreading it out on a baking sheet. Transfer it into dry, clean mason jars after letting it dry out for a few days in a bright location next to a window. This salt tastes great on popcorn, fried eggs, potatoes, and just about anything else. If it lasts that long, it makes a wonderful present and can be kept for a year or more.

8. Herbs Preserved In Salt

Our predecessors could store herbs without expensive eq uipment, such as freezers, and salt-preserving was one of their preferred techniq ues. This method works best with delicate, sensitive herbs that don't dry well. Think about using this technique to preserve basil, cilantro, chives, dill, parsley, or tarragon. All you need is some kosher salt, fresh herbs, and a dry, clean glass jar. Fill the jar to the top by first adding a layer of salt to the bottom, followed by a single layer of herbs, salt, and more herbs. Pull out the herbs as needed, shaking or rinsing the salt off if you'd like, and store the jar in a cool, dark spot, such as a pantry shelf or even the refrigerator. When you're done using the herbs, the salt will still taste like the herbs and can be used in cooking or pickling. Herbs should stay fresh and useable using this preservation method for at least six months and possibly even a year.

9. Herbed Sugar

We make the mistake of assuming that herbs are only used for savory purposes when cooking. The following method of preservation— herb-flavored sugar—shows how cruel this is to herbs. Layer fresh herbs with sugar using the same method as salt-preserving to give the sugar a delicate flavor and preserve the herbs for later use. Herbs can also be finely ground into sugar using a food processor. Think of herbs, like sage, mint, lemon balm, lavender, rosemary, or thyme. Use the glass jar for baking, cooking, and cocktails and store it in a cold, dark location or the refrigerator. Herbs should stay fresh using this method for up to a year.

10. Natural Honey

Honey has antibacterial, antifungal, and antiviral characteristics, making it a natural preservative. Additionally, it can preserve the herbs' flavors for more than a year. The finest honey to use for preserving herbs in honey is local and has a mild flavor (some honey from seasonal flowers will have its flavor). Put your herbs in a clean glass jar, whole or minced, and then cover with honey. Use the infusion to sweeten tea, as a syrup topping, in baking, or even as the foundation for a meat glaze after letting it steep for at least six weeks to allow the flavors to fully meld.

11. Vinegar That Has Been Infused

Herb-infused vinegar is nothing new, but it's a simple method to keep the flavor of your herbs for a long time and makes a nice gift. The secret is to start with lighter vinegar, such as champagne vinegar, white wine vinegar, or other light-hued vinegar. Utilize some herbs and glass canning jars that have been thoroughly cleaned. Distribute the sprigs equally among the jars before covering them with vinegar and allowing at least a quarter-inch of space at the top. Put lids on them and keep them somewhere cool and dark for about a month. Drain the vinegar through a cheesecloth before using to eliminate any sediments. Fill glass bottles with vinegar and, if desired, a decorative sprig or two. These vinegars stay for a very long time and make excellent salad dressings and marinades. As you can see, there are numerous alternatives to drying if you want to extend the season of using your fresh herbs. Never again throw away a harvest or purchase of herbs!

Conclusion

Increase your environment's medicinal plant diversity for health benefits. You now have knowledge about how to develop a medicinal garden in your home, thanks to this book. Knowing which herbs are annuals and perennials will help you plan your herb garden. Learning about each unique herb, its uses, and growing practices is also beneficial in the long run. This will assist you in choosing where to place your plants and how to care for them so that you can enjoy your savory and aromatic herbs for many seasons to come.

THANK YOU!

Dear reader,

I am writing to request that you take a few minutes to leave a review after reading my book. I have put a great deal into creating this work, and it is only with the help of thoughtful feedback from readers like yourself that I can continue to refine and improve my writing. So if you have enjoyed my book, I would be truly grateful if you could take a moment to post your thoughts online. Whether you loved it or had a few constructive criticisms, your feedback will help me become a better writer over time. Thank you in advance for your support.

I hope to hear from you soon.

33648998R00136

Jackapoo Dogs

The Complete Owner's Guide

Jackapoo Dogs

The Complete Owner's Guide

Published by ROC Publishing 2014

DISCLAIMER

The information contained herein has been posted in good faith and is to be used for educational purposes only.

The author has made considerable efforts to present accurate and reliable information in this book. However, the author does not take any legal responsibility for the accuracy, completeness, or usefulness of the information herein. The information in this book is not intended to provide specific advice about individual medical or legal questions. This book should not be considered a substitute for a reader's own independent research and evaluation.

This book may contain links or refer to other web sites, and other web sites may refer to this book. Links to web sites outside of this site do not imply endorsement or approval of those sites or the information they contain. The links to other web sites are provided solely as a convenience to users of this site. The author is not responsible for the accuracy of the information, the content, or the policies of such sites, and shall not be liable for any damages or injury arising from the content or use of those sites.

This content may refer to organizations, businesses, and other resources available through government, nonprofit, and commercial entities. Referrals to such entities are provided solely for informational and educational purposes and as a convenience to the user. A referral to a product or service on this web site should not be considered an endorsement or recommendation of that product or service. The author shall not be liable for any damages or injury arising from the use of or connection with such products, services, or entities.

Foreword

The Jackapoo is a charming combination of the Jack Russell terrier and the poodle. These medium-sized dogs are full of fun and energy, making them an excellent family-friendly pet. If you have ever considered owning one of these dogs as a pet you should learn everything you can about them. That is where this book comes in. Written in a clear and easy-to-read fashion, this book provides you with all the information you need to determine whether a Jackapoo is the right pet for you.

Acknowledgements

Thank you Charlie, Tilly and Zara

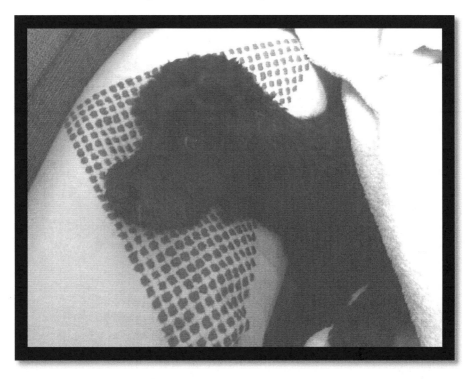

Table of Contents

Chapter One: Introduction   1

   Glossary of Terms   3

Chapter Two: Understanding Jackapoo Dogs   6

   1.) What Are Jackapoo Dogs?   7

   2.) Facts About Jackapoos   9

      Summary of Jackapoo Facts   11

   3.) History of Jackapoo Dogs as Pets   13

   4.) Jack Russell Terrier Facts   15

   5.) Poodle Facts   17

Chapter Three: What to Know Before You Buy   19

   1.) Do You Need a License?   20

      a.) Licensing in the U.S.   20

      b.) Licensing in the U.K.   21

   2.) How Many Should You Buy?   22

   3.) Can Jackapoos Be Kept with Other Pets?   23

   4.) Ease and Cost of Care   24

      a.) Initial Costs   24

      b.) Monthly Costs   28

   5.) Pros and Cons of Jackapoo Dogs   32

Chapter Four: Purchasing Jackapoo Dogs   34

   1.) Where to Buy Jackapoo Dogs   35

a.) Buying in the U.S.   35

b.) Buying in the U.K.   38

2.) Puppy-Proofing Your Home   40

3.) How to Select a Healthy Jackapoo Puppy   43

Chapter Five: Caring for Jackapoo Dogs   46

1.) Habitat Requirements   47

a.) Providing For Your Jackapoo's Needs   47

b.) Creating a Space for Your Jackapoo   50

c.) Meeting Your Jackapoo's Needs for Exercise   51

2.) Feeding Jackapoo Dogs   53

a.) Nutritional Needs   53

b.) Types of Food   55

c.) How Much to Feed   57

3.) Housetraining Your Jackapoo   60

Chapter Six: Breeding Jackapoo Dogs   64

1.) Basic Breeding Info   65

2.) The Breeding Process   67

3.) Raising the Puppies   70

Chapter Seven: Keeping Jackapoos Healthy   74

1.) Common Health Problems   75

2.) Preventing Illness   87

Chapter Eight: Showing Jackapoo Dogs   90

1.) Showing Crossbreed Dogs   91

Scruffts   92

2.) What to Know Before Showing   93

Chapter Nine: Jackapoo Care Sheet   95

1.) Basic Information   96

2.) Cage Set-up Guide   97

3.) Nutritional Information   98

4.) Breeding Tips and Info   99

Chapter Ten: Relevant Websites   101

1.) Food for Jackapoo Dogs   102

2.) Toys and Accessories for Jackapoo Dogs 104

3.) General Info for Dog Care   106

Index   107

Photo Credits   116

References   120

Chapter One: Introduction

If you are looking for a small-breed dog that has a playful attitude and a great deal of intelligence look no further than the Jackapoo. The Jackapoo is a hybrid dog bred from a purebred poodle and a purebred Jack Russell terrier. As a hybrid, the Jackapoo exhibits some of the best qualities and characteristics of both parent breeds. Not only is the Jackapoo breed smart and easy to train, but he makes an excellent family pet.

Before bringing home a new pet, it is always a good idea to learn everything you can about it – this is especially true for the Jackapoo. Caring for a dog is wonderful experience but it can also be challenging at times, so it is essential that you are properly prepared for the task before you go out and buy a puppy. That is where this book comes in.

In this book you will find a wealth of information about the Jackapoo breed including facts about its temperament and tips for proper care. By the time you finish this book you will not only be equipped to make an informed decision regarding whether this is the right breed for you, but you will also be well on your way in preparing your home and your family for your new Jackapoo.

Glossary of Terms

AKC – American Kennel Club; registry of purebred dogs in the United States

Best in Show – the highest award given at a dog show

Bicolor – a coat having two colors, both clearly defined and clearly separated

Bitch – a female dog

Breed Standard – a set of guidelines, often published by a breed club, to ensure uniformity in breeding

Crossbred – a dog whose sire and dam are from two different breeds

Dam – the mother of a dog or litter of puppies

Double Coat – a coat having two layers; typically a soft undercoat and a longer, rough outer coat

Drop Ear – pendulant ears, ears that hang down

Hybrid – the result of crossing two different breeds

Inbreeding – the mating of two dogs that are closely related (i.e. mother to son)

Interbreeding – the mating of two dogs of different breeds

Litter – a group of puppies born at the same time

Neuter – to castrate a male dog or spay a female dog; to render the dog sterile, incapable of breeding

Pedigree – the written record of a dog's genealogy going back at least 3 generations

Prick Ear – ears carried erect, often pointed at the tip

Puppy – a dog under 12 months of age

Purebred – a dog whose dam and sire are of the same breed, both are from unmixed descent

Sire – the male parent of a dog

Small Dog Syndrome – a behavioral condition that often affects small-breed dogs; small dogs may be allowed to perform undesired behaviors (such as barking or jumping) because they are less dangerous than if a larger dog were to perform them; indulgence by owners/lack of training results in dominance and stubbornness in the dog

Stud Dog – a male dog used for breeding purposes

Withers – the tallest point of the body, the ridge between the dog's shoulder blades

Chapter Two: Understanding Jackapoo Dogs

Before you go out and buy a Jackapoo puppy, you would be wise to learn as much as you can about the breed. These dogs make great pets but, like all pets, they require a certain degree of care. In this chapter you will learn the basics about the Jackapoo dog breed including information about the two parent breeds – the standard poodle and the Jack Russell terrier. Once you understand the Jackapoo breed you will be able to decide if it is right for you.

1.) What Are Jackapoo Dogs?

Jackapoo dogs are often referred to as a "designer breed" but, in reality, they are a hybrid breed – a cross between two different breeds. In the case of the Jackapoo, two different purebred dogs are the parents – a toy, miniature or standard Poodle and a Jack Russell terrier. Not all Jackapoos have a 50/50 mix of poodle and Jack Russell blood – it is possible for a Jackapoo to have a greater percentage of one breed than the other and to still be considered a Jackapoo.

Because the percentage of each breed differs from one litter of Jackapoos to another, it is difficult to pinpoint a list of standard qualities or characteristics for the breed. For the most part Jackapoos tend to be very friendly and energetic by nature – they may also be a little bit goofy and they are affectionate with family. Jackapoos are highly intelligent and have a great deal of stamina so they tend to enjoy training for various dog sports including agility and flyball. Most Jackapoos also have a fairly high hunting instinct because both of the parent breeds were originally bred for hunting purposes.

Not all Jackapoos will exhibit the traits just discussed. Personality and temperament varies from one dog to another, regardless of breeding. The best way to gain an understanding of the Jackapoo breed is to learn as much as you can about the two parent breeds – the standard poodle and the Jack Russell terrier. At the end of this chapter you will receive an in-depth overview of both of these breeds to help you understand the Jackapoo a little better.

2.) Facts About Jackapoos

As you've already learned, each Jackapoo is different depending on its breeding. There are, however, certain traits for which the Jackapoo is known – these traits are a combination of the traits exhibited by the parent breeds. For the most part, Jackapoo dogs are very energetic and require a good deal of daily exercise to work off their energy. Because the Jackapoo is also very smart, many owners train them for hunting or various dog sports. The Jackapoo inherits its high stamina and energy from the Jack Russell Terrier side of its heritage and it receives much of its intelligence from the standard poodle.

In terms of appearance, the Jackapoo is a small to medium-sized dog that weighs between 12 and 25 lbs. (5.4 to 11.3 kg) at maturity and measures between 10 and 15 inches (25.4 to 38 cm) tall. These little dogs are generally fairly healthy so, as long as they get enough daily exercise and receive a healthy diet, they can achieve a lifespan between 12 and 15 years. The fact that the Jackapoo is the result of breeding two purebred dogs actually reduces its chances for developing congenital diseases. You will learn more about health concerns for Jackapoos in Chapter Seven.

While every Jackapoo varies slightly in appearance, these dogs generally have a flat head with a medium-length snout and a dark nose. These dogs have long, drop ears that are densely covered in fur, as is the rest of the face. Because the Jackapoo is a mix of the curly-coated poodle and the straight-furred Jack Russell, these dogs often exhibit wavy coats. The coat color varies greatly because poodles come in a wide variety of colors, but a combination of white and tan is common in Jackapoos.

One of the most important thing to keep in mind about Jackapoos is that, despite their small size, they may not be the best choice for apartment dwellers. These dogs have a great deal of energy and they need regular walks and plenty of time outside to work off that energy. If you train your dog for agility or other dog sports to meet his daily exercise needs, however, he may be able to tolerate apartment life. The Jackapoo may be a companion pet but he is by no means a lap dog. Like many small dogs, Jackapoos tend to develop problem behaviors or Small Dog Syndrome if they get bored because they don't receive enough exercise or play time.

Summary of Jackapoo Facts

Origins: unknown, likely developed in the United States

Pedigree: hybrid of the Standard Poodle and Jack Russell Terrier breeds

Weight: 12 to 25 lbs. (5.4 – 11.3 kg)

Height: average 10 to 15 inches (25.4 – 38 cm)

Lifespan: 12 to 15 years

Coat: may be smooth or rough in texture; either straight or curly; often medium-length

Colors: any color; combination of white and tan is most commonly seen

Eyes: large and round; usually dark in color

Ears: medium-length, drop ears

Face: flat head, medium-length muzzle, un-tapered

Temperament: energetic, affectionate with family, alert and outgoing; generally good with kids; intelligent

Strangers: may be wary around strangers, make good watchdogs

Other Dogs: generally good with other dogs

Other Pets: strong hunting instincts, may not be good with small household pets

Training: very intelligent, responds well to firm and consistent training (best if started early)

Energy: fairly high exercise requirements; daily walk is required plus plenty of play time

3.) History of Jackapoo Dogs as Pets

The history of the Jackapoo breed is largely unknown because hybridization of purebred dogs is a practice that has existed for many years. While the origins of many purebred dogs can be traced back to a single breeder or a collection of kennels, the origins of the Jackapoo are unknown – no single breeder or kennel is credited with the development of the breed. What is known is that the breed likely originate in the United States.

To better understand the Jackapoo, you may be interested in learning a little bit about the history of the parent breeds. The standard poodle's origins can be traced back to the 15th and 16th centuries in Germany where it was called the Pudelhund. These dogs were commonly used as water retrievers or gun dogs in a variety of bird-hunting applications. Eventually the Pudelhund was bred into three different sizes – standard, miniature, and toy. The AKC currently recognizes the poodle in all three sizes as a single breed within the Non-Sporting Group.

The Jack Russell Terrier's origins can be traced back to Reverend John Russell, a parson who also happened to be a hunting enthusiast, during the early 1800s. The Jack Russell Terrier was bred from a now-extinct breed called the English White Terrier. Because hunters during the time found it difficult to differentiate between the dog and its prey in the field it became necessary to develop a mostly white dog. Thus, the Jack Russell Terrier was developed from a small white-and-tan terrier.

4.) Jack Russell Terrier Facts

The Jack Russell is a small terrier breed that grows between 10 and 15 inches (25 to 38 cm) tall and weighs between 4 and 18 lbs. (6.4 to 8.2 kg) at maturity. These little dogs have a great deal of energy and they love having a job to perform. Originally bred for hunting foxes, these dogs have a strong prey drive and a great deal of stamina. Simply put, these dogs can be hard to keep up with at times and they require a great deal of daily exercise. For this reason, many Jack Russell Terrier owners train their dogs for either hunting or various dog sports.

Jack Russell terriers are predominately white in color, though most exhibit some level of black or tan coloring on various parts of the body – primarily the ears, face, and tail. These dogs may have either a smooth or rough coat – some even exhibit a combination of the two, known as a broken coat. Jack Russells have small v-shaped ears that are carried forward on the head and though they may prick up when the dog is alert, they are actually drop ears.

In terms of temperament, the Jack Russell terrier is a made to work – these dogs thrive when giving a job to do and they tend to develop problem behaviors if they become bored due to lack of exercise or mental stimulation. Jack Russell terriers can be stubborn or strong-willed at times so early socialization and training is very important for this breed. As long as they are socialized properly, this breed can be friendly toward children but they will not tolerate abuse. For this reason, they are only recommended for families with older children who understand how to properly treat a dog.

5.) Poodle Facts

The poodle is widely regarded as one of the most intelligent dog breeds. Though it was originally bred as a water retriever, these dogs excel in a variety of hunting applications and many different dog sports including agility, tracking, obedience, and even herding. There are three different sizes of poodle – standard, miniature, and toy. The standard poodle stands over 15 inches (38 cm tall) while the miniature poodle stands between 10 and 15 inches (25.4 to 38 cm) tall. The toy poodle stands under 10 inches (25.4) tall at maturity.

In terms of appearance, the poodle is an elegant and active breed. These dogs have a square build with a tapered muzzle and a dark nose. The drop ears fold over very close to the head and they are set at or just below eye level. A poodle's coat is naturally curly and dense, though many poodle owners clip the coat short. Unlike many dogs, poodles do not have a double coat – they have a single-layer coat of minimally-shedding fur. For this reason, poodles are often considered hypoallergenic, a good choice for people who suffer from allergies.

The poodle's coat comes in a wide variety of colors and they may be either solid- or parti-colored. Some of the most common colors include white, black, brown, gray, apricot, red, cream, and sable. Parti-colored poodles typically have a white coat with solid-colored patches. In terms of temperament, the poodle is very friendly by nature but may be reserved around strangers. These dogs make great family pets, especially for families with children. Because poodles are so intelligent, they require plenty of mental stimulation in addition to daily exercise to prevent them from becoming bored and developing problem behaviors.

Chapter Three: What to Know Before You Buy

Now that you understand the basics about the Jackapoo you may have a better idea whether these dogs are the right pet for you. Before you make your decision, however, there are some additional factors to consider. In this chapter you will receive information about licensing your Jackapoo, adding a Jackapoo to a multi-pet household, and the pros and cons of the breed. By the time you finish this chapter you should be able to make an informed decision regarding whether Jackapoos are the right breed for you.

1.) Do You Need a License?

Bringing home a new pet can be an exciting experience, but don't let your excitement get the best of you – there are a few practical things you need to take care of. One of the most important things you need to determine before bringing your Jackapoo home is whether or not you need a license to keep him. Licensing requirements vary from one country to another, and from one state to another, so be sure to check with your local council so you don't incur a hefty fine.

a.) Licensing in the U.S.

In the United States there is no federal requirement for licensing your dog – licensing requirements are decided at the state level. Before you bring home a Jackapoo you need to determine whether a license is required in your state to keep a dog – you can find this information by contacting your local council. You can also ask your local veterinarian or the breeder from whom you purchase your Jackapoo for information as well.

Even if your state does not require you to license your dog, it is always a good idea to do so anyway. A dog license only costs about $25 (£16.25) (renewable each year) and it adds an extra level of protection if your dog happens to get lost. If your dog carries proper identification, anyone who finds him will be able to contact you to reunite you with your pet. Keep in mind that dog licenses typically require a current rabies vaccine so make sure you have proof of your dog's vaccination when you apply for a license.

b.) Licensing in the U.K.

It is mandatory for dog owners to license their dogs in the United Kingdom. The only exceptions to this rules are police dogs and assistance dogs – puppies can also get by without a license until they reach 6 months of age as long as the owner owns the mother as well. Just as is true in the U.S., dog licenses in the U.K. are renewable annually. You do not, however require a rabies vaccination because rabies has been eradicated in the U.K.

2.) How Many Should You Buy?

The answer to this question is not a simple "yes" or "no" for a variety of reasons. For one thing, your ability to provide for more than one dog is a key factor in deciding whether you should keep more than one Jackapoo. Jackapoos are a high-energy dog that requires a great deal of time, attention, and training. So, unless you have enough time to fully devote yourself to two dogs, you may want to stick with just one.

Another factor to consider is the fact that Jackapoos become bored easily. These dogs are very smart and highly active, so if they do not receive enough daily exercise and mental stimulation they may become bored and could develop problem behaviors. In some cases, having a second dog around may give your Jackapoo the extra attention it needs when you are not around to keep him occupied.

3.) *Can Jackapoos Be Kept with Other Pets?*

For the most part, Jackapoos get along with other dogs as long as they are introduced while still young. Socialization plays a key role in your Jackapoo's ability to get along with other pets. It is important to keep in mind that, as friendly or gentle as your Jackapoo may seem, he was bred from two hunting breeds so he has a very high natural prey drive. This means that he may have a tendency to chase cats and small household pets. Never leave your Jackapoo alone with other pets and be very careful if you choose to introduce them to each other.

4.) Ease and Cost of Care

Before you make your final decision regarding whether a Jackapoo is the right pet for you, you need to think about whether you can cover the financial burden of owning a dog. Becoming a Jackapoo owner can be fairly expensive – not only do you have to purchase the dog and all of the necessary accessories, but you also have to keep up with monthly costs for food and veterinary care. In this section you will receive an overview of the initial costs and monthly costs for keeping a Jackapoo.

a.) Initial Costs

The initial costs for keeping a Jackapoo dog include the following: the purchase price, spay/neuter surgery, microchipping, vaccinations, crate, and other accessories. Below you will find an overview of each expense as well as an estimated cost range:

Purchase Price

The purchase price for Jackapoo puppies may vary greatly from one breeder to another. The important thing to remember is that Jackapoos are technically a hybrid breed, so you should not be paying purebred prices. Any breeder that attempts to sell you a Jackapoo for more than $500 (£325) is likely only in the business for the profit. You should plan to spend between $200 and $400 (£130 to £260) for a Jackapoo puppy.

Spay/Neuter Surgery

If you do not plan to breed your Jackapoo, you should definitely plan to have him or her neutered or spayed to prevent unwanted pregnancies. Spaying and neutering your Jackapoo may also reduce his risk for developing certain diseases. If you go to a licensed veterinarian, spay/neuter surgery could cost you several hundred dollars. If you look around, however, you should be able to find a low-cost clinic that is run through a local shelter or rescue agency that will perform neuter surgery for $50 to $100 (£32.50 - £65) and spay surgery for about $100 to $200 (£65 - £130).

Microchipping

Microchipping is not a required expense, but it is highly recommended. Having your dog carry proper identification is a great way to increase your chances of finding him should he get lost. If your dog loses his collar, however, that identification is worthless. A microchip is a small device implanted in the dog's skin that carries a number – that number is linked to the owner's contact information. If your pet is found, the microchip can be scanned to find your information to reunite you with your pet. Microchipping only takes a few minutes and the procedure generally costs under $30 (£19.50) to perform.

Vaccinations

If you purchase your Jackapoo from a licensed breeder, the puppy will likely already have a few vaccinations under his belt. Over the first few weeks that you have your puppy at home, however, you will need to take him in to the vet to complete is puppy vaccines. The cost of these vaccines may vary depending where you go and how many your puppy needs. You should plan to spend about $50 (£32.50) for initial vaccinations just to be prepared.

Crate

Having a crate for your Jackapoo puppy is essential for housebreaking. The crate should ideally only be large enough for your puppy to sit, stand, lie down, and turn around comfortably – if there is too much extra space your puppy may end up having accidents in the crate. You should plan to spend about $30 (£19.50) for a puppy crate.

Other Accessories

In addition to the costs discussed above, there are a few other expenses you may need to cover before bringing your Jackapoo puppy home. You will need to provide food and water bowls for your puppy as well as some kind of blanket or plush dog bed to line the puppy's crate. You should also stock up on a variety of toys to keep your puppy's chewing under control and to use during play time. To be on the safe side, budget about $100 (£65) for these extra costs.

Initial Costs for Jackapoo Dogs		
Cost	**One Dog**	**Two Dogs**
Purchase Price	$200 to $400 (£130 - £260)	$400 to $800 (£260 - £520)
Spay/Neuter	$50 to $200 (£32.50 - £130)	$100 to $400 (£65 - £260)
Microchipping	$30 (£19.50)	$60 (£39)
Vaccinations	$50 (£32.50)	$100 (£65)

Crate	$30 (£19.50)	$60 (£39)
Accessories	$100 (£65)	$200 (£130)
Total	$460 to $810 (£300 – £527)	$920 to $1,620 (£600 - £1,053)

b.) Monthly Costs

Once you bring your Jackapoo home, your wallet does not get much of a break. You will have to cover monthly costs for food, veterinary care, grooming, license renewal, and other costs. <u>Below you will find an overview of each expense as well as an estimated cost range</u>:

Food and Treats

Jackapoo dogs are a small to medium-sized breed, so you should not expect exorbitant monthly food expenses. It is, however, important that you select a high-quality dog food rather than settling for a cheap brand. Plan to spend about $25 (£16) on a large bag of dog food that will last you at least one month. In addition to food, budget about $10 (£6.50) per month extra for treats.

Veterinary Care

Providing your Jackapoo with regular veterinary care is extremely important. While your Jackapoo is still a puppy he may need to see the vet every few months to catch up on vaccines. Once he reaches a year old, however, he should only need two visits per year. The average cost for a vet visit is about $40 (£26). If you plan for two visits each year and divide the cost over 12 months, you are left with a monthly cost of about $7 (£4.55).

In addition to routine visits, you will also have to cover the cost of monthly medications recommended by your vet. These medications include heartworm preventives and topical flea and tick preventives. The combined cost for these treatments should be about $15 (£9.75) a month. Added to the $7 (£4.55) per month cost for vet visits, you are left with a total of about $22 (£14.30) per month for veterinary care.

Grooming

Because Jackapoos have poodle blood in them, they have medium-length curly coats that require a good bit of grooming. A visit to the groomer for a Jackapoo will cost anywhere between $50 and $90 (£32.50 – £58.50) depending on the type of cut you choose. In addition to brushing your Jackapoo several times a week, he will require professional grooming 3 to 4 times per year. Divided over the course of 12 months, the average monthly cost for grooming your Jackapoo will be between $17 and $30 (£11 - £19.50)

License Renewal

You are only required to renew your Jackapoo's license once a year and the average cost for license renewal is only about $25 (£16.25) per year which averages to about $2 (£1.30) per month.

Other Costs

In addition to the costs discussed above, you should plan for unexpected costs as well. These costs may not occur every month, but it is always a good idea to have some extra money set aside just in case they do come up. Some unexpected costs you may need to cover include replacement toys, new collars as your Jackapoo grows, cleaning products, and more. To be on the safe side, you should budget about $15 (£9.75) for extra costs.

Monthly Costs for Jackapoo Dogs		
Cost	**One Dog**	**Two Dogs**
Food/Treats	$35 (£22.75)	$70 (£45.50)
Veterinary Care	$22 (£14.30)	$44 (£28.60)
Grooming	$17 to $30 (£11 - £19.50)	$34 to $60 (£22.10 - £39)
License Renewal	$2 (£1.30)	$4 (£2.60)
Other Costs	$15 (£9.75)	$30 (£19.50)
Total	$91 to $104 (£59 - £68)	$182 to $208 (£118 - £135)

5.) Pros and Cons of Jackapoo Dogs

Jackapoos make great companion pets, but they may not be the right choice for everyone. Before you go out and buy a Jackapoo you would be wise to learn the pros and cons about the breed. You will find a list of pros and cons for Jackapoo dogs below:

Pros for Jackapoos

- Small to medium-sized breed, only weighs up to 25 lbs. (11.5 kg).
- Generally very friendly and affectionate by nature – makes a good family pet.
- Can get along with children if properly socialized and introduced at a young age.
- Very intelligent – generally responds well to firm and consistent training.
- Responds well to training for hunting and various dog sports including agility and flyball.
- Fairly low shedding, though coat requires regular grooming and maintenance.
- Generally a healthy breed, less susceptible to congenital conditions than purebred dogs.

Cons for Jackapoos

- Very high-energy breed, requires a good deal of daily exercise and mental stimulation.
- Can be wary around strangers unless properly socialized.
- May be impatient with young children – must be supervised.
- High prey drive, may not be a good choice for homes with cats and other household pets.
- May develop problem behaviors if not properly exercised.

Chapter Four: Purchasing Jackapoo Dogs

Now that you've made the decision that a Jackapoo dog is right for you and your family, you can move one to the practical aspects of purchasing and raising your puppy. In this chapter you will receive some practical information about finding a Jackapoo breeder, puppy-proofing your home, and selecting a healthy Jackapoo puppy. By the time you finish this chapter you will be ready and equipped to start your search.

1.) *Where to Buy Jackapoo Dogs*

Once you've decided that you do indeed want to purchase a Jackapoo puppy, your next step is to find a reputable breeder. You should not go out and buy a puppy from the first Jackapoo breeder you find – it is important that you take the time to evaluate the breeder, as well as the available puppies, before you buy. In this section you will receive insight into finding a Jackapoo dog breeder in both the United States and the United Kingdom.

a.) Buying in the U.S.

In order to ensure a healthy litter of puppies, breeders much select two healthy parent dogs. In the case of the Jackapoo, this means a healthy poodle and a healthy Jack Russell terrier. Because Jackapoos are a hybrid breed, breeders need to have experience and expertise with both parent breeds to ensure a healthy litter of puppies. Do an internet search or ask around at your local pet store or veterinarian's office for recommendations of Jackapoo breeders. Once you've compiled a list of breeders you can go through them to determine which one is the best option to buy a Jackapoo puppy from.

After you've compiled your list of breeders, go through the following steps to narrow down the list:

1. Assemble as much information about each breeder as you can – visit their website and search for reviews online.

2. Contact each breeder and ask some general questions regarding their experience with Jackapoos (and the parent breeds) as well as their breeding experience.

3. Ask each breeder about their breeding program including the efforts they take to avoid the passing of congenital diseases.

4. Eliminate breeders from your list if you are not satisfied with their answers to your questions – if the breeder doesn't seem knowledgeable and experienced, or if he refuses to answer your questions, take him off the list.

5. Schedule a visit to each of the remaining breeders on your list and ask for a tour of the breeding facilities.

6. Take a look around to make sure that everything is clean and well-kept – ask to see the breeding stock to ensure that they are in good condition.

7. Select the breeder that you feel is the most responsible and experienced – do not just pick the first one you visit unless that breeder truly is the best option.

8. Put down a deposit for a puppy to reserve one from the next litter. Later in this chapter you will receive advice for selecting a healthy puppy.

Now that you know how to go about finding a reputable Jackapoo breeder, here are a few links you might try to receive more information:

U.S. Jackapoo Breeders:

StarView Farm.
<http://www.starview.macmate.me/Jackapoo/Home.html>

KNS Pups.

<http://www.knspups.com/jackapoo_past_puppies.htm>

Laughlin Kennel.

<http://laughlinkennel.com/jackapoo.html>

Dan's Jackapoo Puppies.

<http://jackapoo.danbye.net/>

b.) Buying in the U.K.

Finding a Jackapoo breeder in the U.K. is the same as it is in the U.S. You can perform and online search for breeders in your area or consult your local rescue organization or veterinarian's office for recommendations. If you are not concerned about having a Jackapoo puppy, consider placing a request with a local shelter or rescue organization for them to let you know if a Jackapoo dog comes in. Adopting a rescue dog is an excellent option if you do not want to deal with the hassle of raising a puppy. Rescue dogs may be a little older but they are typically already housebroken and may have some training as well. Plus, adopting a rescue dog gives a homeless pet a new forever home and he will be forever grateful to you.

U.K. Jackapoo Breeders:

Doodle Dogs.

<http://www.doodledogsderby.co.uk/>

UK Kennel Club Breeders Directory.

<http://www.thekennelclub.org.uk/getting-a-dog-or-puppy/finding-the-right-dog/>

Trovit.co.uk.

<http://products.trovit.co.uk/pets/jackapoo-puppies>

2.) Puppy-Proofing Your Home

Before you bring your Jackapoo puppy home you need to prepare the house. Not only do you need to set up a little area of the house for your puppy's crate and food bowls, but you also need to take steps to protect your puppy from potential dangers. Below you will find a list of tips for puppy-proofing your home:

- Keep all food stored in the refrigerator, pantry, or in cupboards – any food left out needs to be in tight-lidded containers.

- Store all cleaning products and chemicals in a secure cabinet where your puppy cannot access it – look into child-proof cabinet closures.

- Keep all of your medications (over-the-counter and prescription) stored away in drawers or in the medicine cabinet.

- Make sure your trash cans all have lids or store them under the sink where your puppy can't get to it.

- Check all of the houseplants you keep in the house (as well as the plants in your yard) to make sure they aren't toxic to dogs.

- Tie up loose blinds and electrical cords – cover unused outlets with plastic covers.

- Keep all small objects (including socks and small articles of clothing) put away where your puppy can't chew on them – they may be a choking hazard.

- Make sure all doors and windows to the outside are closed or otherwise secured so your puppy cannot wander off.

- Keep doors closed or use baby gates to keep your puppy out of areas of the house that might be dangerous – this includes the garage, rooms with small objects, even the kitchen during cooking.

- If you have a cat, make sure the litter box is stored somewhere your puppy cannot reach it.

- Avoid using tobacco products in the house – if you must, do so outside and make sure to properly dispose of everything.

- Consider fencing an area of your yard where your puppy can run free if your entire yard isn't fenced already.

- Keep all bodies of water covered because they are a drowning risk – this includes toilet bowls, bathtubs, and outdoor ponds or pools.

Note: In addition to puppy-proofing your home, you should also make sure to supervise your puppy when he is out of his crate. Ideally, you should keep your puppy confined to whatever room you are in rather than giving him free reign of the house.

3.) How to Select a Healthy Jackapoo Puppy

Not only do you need to go through a selection process for choosing a reputable Jackapoo breeder, but you also need to take your time in choosing a Jackapoo puppy. The more careful you are in selecting your puppy to make sure he is healthy, the less likely you are to have to deal with expensive medical problems down the line. The last thing you want to do is rush the process then bring home a Jackapoo puppy who isn't in good condition – the puppy may get sick or even die.

Follow these steps to select a healthy Jackapoo puppy once you have already chosen your breeder:

1. Inquire about the age of the puppies – the best time to buy a puppy is when it has already been weaned and when it has had a few weeks of socialization (between 8 and 12 weeks).

2. Step back and watch the puppies interact with each other for a few minutes – you should also gauge their reaction to you as well.

3. Watch for signs of fear or nervousness when you approach the puppies – some nervousness is to be expected but puppies that have been properly socialized will not be scared or aggressive at your approach.

4. Check for signs of healthy activity – they puppies should be eager to play (with each other and with you), not laying around looking sick.

5. Let the puppies come up and give you a good sniff and a lick or two before you try to handle them – handle one puppy at a time.

6. Interact with the puppy by playing with him for a few minutes to get a feel for his temperament and personality.

7. During this time you can also perform a basic check for physical symptoms of disease.

8. Check for signs of swelling or discharge around the nose, mouth, eyes, and ears – if there is an odor coming from the ears or a lot of buildup, the puppy could have an ear infection.

9. Run your hands over the puppies body to check for lumps and bumps – if the puppy yelps when you touch him, check for signs of illness or injury in the sensitive area.

10. Watch the puppies eat, if you can, to make sure that they have a healthy appetite.

11. Check the facility for signs of diarrhea – chronic diarrhea is not only a symptom of disease but it can lead to dehydration and a number of other health problems.

12. Select a healthy puppy that you get along with and speak to the breeder about putting down a deposit, if you haven't done so already.

Note: A reputable Jackapoo breeder won't let you take home a puppy that is younger than 8 weeks. Some states even have laws which prohibit the sale of puppies under 8 weeks of age. It is important to wait until the puppy is fully weaned and eating solid food before you bring him home.

Chapter Five: Caring for Jackapoo Dogs

Caring for your Jackapoo requires more than just giving him a bowl of food now and then and letting him outside. Before you buy a Jackapoo you need to have a basic understanding of his habitat requirements and his nutritional needs. You will find this information in this chapter as well as a step-by-step guide for housebreaking your Jackapoo puppy.

1.) Habitat Requirements

Owning a dog is not the same as keeping a hamster or some other pet that lives most of its life in a cage or enclosure. While your Jackapoo should have a crate in which you keep him overnight and during long absences, he will largely be given free reign of the house. Even so, your Jackapoo needs to feel like there is a certain area of the house that he can call his own. It is in this area that you should place his crate along with his food and water dishes and his toys.

a.) Providing For Your Jackapoo's Needs

Below you will find a list of the things you need to provide for your Jackapoo as well as an overview of each item:

- Crate or kennel (see Section 1 of this chapter)
- Soft blanket or dog bed (see Section 1 of this chapter)
- Food and water dishes
- Assortment of toys
- Collar, leash, and harness
- Grooming supplies
- Outdoor space

Food and Water Dishes

You don't have to spend a small fortune on your Jackapoo's food and water bowls – quality is more important than appearance. Perhaps the best thing you can do is to simply buy a set of stainless steel bowls. Stainless steel is easy to clean and it is less likely to harbor bacteria than ceramic or plastic bowls. Bowls made of stainless steel will also hold up well if you happen to drop one or if your Jackapoo gets excited and knocks one over.

Assortment of Toys

Having an assortment of toys available is especially important for Jackapoo puppies – while your puppy is teething he will have the urge to chew on everything he sees. Even adult Jackapoos need a good toy or two to play with to work off some excess energy. Some toys even provide a means of mental stimulation which is also incredibly important for an intelligent breed like the Jackapoo. In addition to having ropes and squeaky toys, you should provide your Jackapoo with a Kong toy or some other toy that provides mental stimulation. Keep in mind that you can make some dog toys yourself with items you already have around the house rather than spending a small fortune on things your dog will chew up in a week.

Collar, Leash and Harness

These three items are incredibly important and you may need to replace them once in a while as your Jackapoo puppy grows. It is incredibly important that you choose a collar that is the right size for your Jackapoo – if you don't choose the right size it may not fit right and it could either slip off easily or restrict your puppy's breathing. Collar sizing is generally done by weight, so check the label to determine which size is best for your Jackapoo and remember that you'll have to replace it as he grows.

In addition to a collar that your Jackapoo will wear all the time, you should also invest in a good leash and harness. A harness is a great option to have for when you are walking your dog. Not only does a harness take the pressure off your Jackapoo's neck, but it also gives you greater control – this is important if your Jackapoo has a tendency to pull while he is on the leash. As is true with collars, harness sizing is generally done by weight so read the label carefully to make sure you get the right size.

Grooming Supplies

Because the Jackapoo is a mix of a Jack Russell and a standard poodle, these dogs have medium-length coats of curly or wavy hair. This being the case, Jackapoos require frequent brushing and grooming. You should plan to brush your Jackapoo several times a week using a slicker brush or a wire-pin brush to work out tangles and to remove dead hair. You will need to have your Jackapoo professionally groomed 3 to 4 times a year to have his fur trimmed as well.

Outdoor Space

Because Jackapoos are bred from two very active breeds, they have a lot of energy and require a great deal of daily exercise. In addition to a long daily walk or jog, Jackapoos need some outdoor space in which they can run and play. Ideally, your outdoor space should be fenced so your Jackapoo cannot escape – you may be surprised at how well they are able to burrow under fences or get around gates. If you keep your Jackapoo outside for extended periods of time make sure to give him access to fresh water and shelter. In the summer, your Jackapoo needs to have access to shade so he does not develop heat stroke.

b.) Creating a Space for Your Jackapoo

Using your Jackapoo's crate, food/water dish, and toys, you can create a small section of your house for him to call his own. Choose an area of the house that is quiet and not in the middle of things in case your Jackapoo needs a break and wants a place to rest quietly. You should not, however, select an area that is so far removed from the main activity of the house that your dog feels neglected. When you are away from home you will need to confine your Jackapoo to his crate until he is fully crate trained. After that point, however, you may choose to let him roam freely in the house or confine him to his special area. It is important that you never use the crate or his area as punishment – it needs to be a place where he WANTS to go.

c.) Meeting Your Jackapoo's Needs for Exercise

As it has already been mentioned, the Jackapoo is an incredibly active breed. Both parent breeds, the poodle and the Jack Russell terrier, were originally bred for hunting and they have a great deal of physical and mental stamina. You should plan to provide your Jackapoo with a 30-minute walk once a day in addition to plenty of playtime and outdoor time, when possible. In addition to giving your Jackapoo a walk you can play mentally stimulating games with him such as fetch or hide-and-seek.

Another option to meet your Jackapoo's need for exercise is to train him for some type of dog sport. There are many dog sports to choose from including agility, obedience, flyball, disc dog, and more – feel free to try a few to see which your dog likes best. Training your dog for dog sports is not only a great way to give him some extra exercise, but it also helps to increase the bond between you and your pet. You may find that you get as much enjoyment out of the activity as your Jackapoo does!

2.) Feeding Jackapoo Dogs

Because the Jackapoo is a hybrid of the poodle and Jack Russell terrier breeds, his nutritional needs are a little tough to calculate. The Jackapoo is a medium-sized breed by nature, so plan to follow the feeding recommendations for other breeds of this size. In this chapter you will receive an overview of general nutritional needs for dogs and tips for making considerations especially for your Jackapoo. You will also receive tips for choosing a dog food and for feeding your Jackapoo the right amount.

a.) Nutritional Needs

In order to understand the nutritional needs of your Jackapoo, you may first want to learn about the dietary requirements of the poodle and the Jack Russell terrier. <u>Below you will find a brief overview of the nutritional needs for these parent breeds</u>:

Nutritional Needs for Poodles

- Young poodles need a lean, high-calorie diet
- Diet should be rich in animal protein (chicken or fish)

- Carbs, vitamins, and minerals should come from plant sources
- Processed grains should generally be avoided
- Older poodles require fewer calories as their activity level decreases

Nutritional Needs for Jack Russell Terriers

- Require more protein and calories than similar-sized dog breeds
- Protein should come from animal sources (such as meat or fish)
- Balance of plants and grains for carbohydrates, vitamins and minerals

Given these nutritional profiles, you can see some similarities between the two breeds. It is safe to assume, then, that those similarities hold true for the Jackapoo breed. Using the information above, you should plan to give your Jackapoo a diet that is rich in animal proteins as well as animal fats but low in processed grains. Your Jackapoo should get a majority of his carbohydrates, vitamins, and minerals from high-quality plant sources, not from processed grains.

b.) Types of Food

Now that you know the basic nutritional needs of your Jackapoo you can start to consider what type of food you want to feed him. It is essential that your Jackapoo receive a balance of macronutrients (protein, fats, and carbs) and micronutrients (vitamins and minerals), so you must choose a high-quality dog food formula. In order to make sure that the type of food you choose will meet your dog's basic nutritional needs, look for the AAFCO statement of nutritional adequacy.

AAFCO stands for the American Association of Feed Control Officials and it is a group of local, state, and federal agencies that are in charge of monitoring and regulating the production of animal feed – this includes pet food. Dog food products that display the AAFCO statement of nutritional adequacy have undergone testing to ensure that they meet the basic nutritional needs of dogs in certain life stages – growth and reproduction (puppies or pregnant/lactating females) or adult maintenance. If the dog food meets these needs, you will see the following statement displayed on the package:

"(Product Name) is formulated to meet the nutritional levels established by the AAFCO Dog Food Nutrient Profiles"

If the product does not meet AAFCO standards, it may sport a statement like *"This product is intended for intermittent or supplemental feeding only."* This may be the case with dog treats as opposed to dog food. When shopping for dog food, you should only purchase formulas that show the AAFCO statement of nutritional adequacy. <u>After you check for that statement, however, there are still a few things you should look for, including the following</u>:

- A high-quality source of animal protein listed first on the ingredient list (chicken, turkey, fish, etc.)

- Sources of digestible carbohydrate (cooked rice, oats, barley, etc.)

- An absence of common allergens like wheat and corn (Poodles are particularly sensitive to food allergies)

- A lack of filler ingredients like byproducts that do not add much nutritional value

- Important minerals dog need include calcium, phosphorus, potassium, magnesium, iron, copper and manganese

- Important vitamins dogs need include Vitamin A, Vitamin A, Vitamin B-12, Vitamin D, Vitamin C

c.) How Much to Feed

The amount you feed your Jackapoo will vary depending on several factors including his age, size, and activity level. When your Jackapoo is a puppy, he will need to eat more frequently than when he is an adult to fuel his growth and development. Once your Jackapoo reaches maturity you should stick to a regular feeding schedule and avoid overfeeding so he does not become obese. Dogs that engage in regular exercise and those that are trained for dog sports may need more food and/or more frequent feedings than dogs that lead a sedentary lifestyle.

The size of the Jackapoo can be deceiving in terms of his energy needs. What many dog owners do not realize is that small dogs actually need more calories than larger dogs due to an increased rate of metabolism. This is especially true for a naturally active breed like the Jackapoo. Jack Russell terriers have a higher requirement for protein and calories than other dogs their size, as do poodles. Thus, it is safe to assume that the Jackapoo has similar requirements.

In order to determine how much you should feed your Jackapoo, you need to check the dog food label. Different formulas have different calories, so check the feeding recommendations as a place to start. Ideally, you should feed puppies freely to support their growth, but adult dogs should receive their food divided into two portions (one in the morning and one in the evening works best). The feeding recommendations on the food label will likely be calculated by weight, so you'll need to know how much your Jackapoo weighs.

Start by feeding the amount recommended and monitor your Jackapoo's weight and energy over the next two to three weeks. If your Jackapoo loses weight or appears to be sluggish, slightly increase his daily ration. If your Jackapoo gains weight, slightly decrease his daily ration. Make small changes at a time and monitor your Jackapoo for at least a week or two after each change to see what the results are. If you need more help formulating a healthy diet for your Jackapoo, consult your veterinarian.

3.) Housetraining Your Jackapoo

Many inexperienced dog owners mistakenly believe that housebreaking a dog is difficult. While it does require a certain level of commitment, housetraining for a Jackapoo is not hard. If you are firm and consistent in your training methods you could have a fully housebroken Jackapoo in a matter of 2 to 3 weeks. The best method for fast housetraining is the crate training method. This method involves keeping your Jackapoo confined to a crate overnight and when you are not at home – this reduces his chances for having an accident.

The reasoning behind this principle is simple – dogs do not like to soil their beds. If you purchase a crate that is just large enough for your Jackapoo to comfortably sit, stand, lie down, and turn around, he will regard the crate as his bed and any time he is in it he will have a natural aversion to soiling. As long as you give your Jackapoo plenty of opportunities to do his business when he is not in the crate, you should have no trouble at all with housebreaking.

<u>Follow these steps to crate train your Jackapoo</u>:

- Select a crate that is just large enough for your Jackapoo to comfortably sit, stand, lie down, and turn around in.

- Line the crate with a soft blanket or a plush dog bed to make it more comfortable for your dog.

- Confine your Jackapoo to the crate overnight and when you are away from home – do not leave any food or water in the crate with him but offer him water as soon as you let him out.

- When you let your puppy out of the crate, immediately take him outside to do his business.

- Select a certain area of the yard where you want your Jackapoo to do his business – this makes cleanup much easier on your part and makes training easier as well.

- When you take your Jackapoo outside, lead him directly to that area and tell him to "go pee" or give a similar command.

- When your dog responds appropriately, praise and reward him then take him back inside.

- While you are at home, keep your Jackapoo in the same room as you and keep an eye out for signs that he has to go – if he starts to squat, clap your hands loudly to distract him then immediately take him outside.

- Take your Jackapoo outside every hour or two while you are at home – especially after meals and playtime.

- Confine your Jackapoo to the crate overnight only in increments of 3 hours to start.

- As your Jackapoo gets older, he will be able to hold his bladder for longer periods of time – eventually you will be able to crate him all night.

*Note: It is important that you do not give your Jackapoo reason to believe that placing him in the crate is a punishment. If you use the crate correctly, your Jackapoo will come to see it as a little space to call his own and he will go there when he needs some quiet time or wants to rest. Do not force your Jackapoo to stay in the crate for longer than he can hold his bladder – if you work during the day, make sure you have a friend or family member stop by to let your Jackapoo out and to give him a few minutes of play time before he goes back in.

Chapter Six: Breeding Jackapoo Dogs

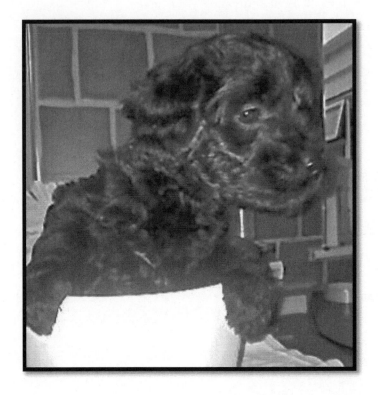

Breeding dogs can be an exciting challenge, but it is definitely not something you should take on lightly. Before you decide to breed your Jackapoos, take the time to learn everything you can about the breeding process. Only if you are sure you are able to provide for your pregnant dog and the puppies properly should you breed your Jackapoo.

1.) Basic Breeding Info

Before breeding your Jackapoo dogs, you need to think long and hard about why you are doing it. Breeding can be risky for the female dog so unless you have experience or you are able to provide veterinary supervision, you may want to skip breeding entirely. Many dog owners mistakenly believe that breeding their dog is a good way to make some extra money. In reality, the cost of caring for the pregnant dog and raising the puppies until they can be sold is often more than the price you would fetch for the litter.

If you do not plan to breed your Jackapoo, you need to have him or her neutered or spayed before the dog reaches 6 months of age. Female Jack Russell terriers typically go into their first heat between 6 and 12 months of age and then they will have a heat cycle every 6 months thereafter. Male Jack Russells can reach sexual maturity a little earlier than females, often around 5 months of age. The same is true for male and female poodles, so you should expect your Jackapoo to reach sexual maturity around 5 months for males and between 6 and 12 months for females.

Even though females are capable of becoming pregnant during their first heat, Jack Russell breeders recommended that you wait until the dog is 1 year old to breed her. Poodle breeders often recommend waiting until the female is 2 years old to breed her. Because Jackapoos are a cross between these two breeds, the ideal breeding age is a little fuzzy – you should plan to wait at least 12 months, however. There is less risk for male dogs when it comes to breeding, so they can be bred any time after they reach sexual maturity, though most breeders recommend waiting until he is 9 to 12 months old.

The average heat cycle lasts about 21 days and pregnancy can occur at any time during the female's heat cycle. The female dog is going to be most fertile, however, about 1 week into her cycle. Once the female becomes pregnant she carries the puppies for a period of time known as the gestation period. For most dogs this period lasts for about 63 days but poodles typically have a gestation period between 59 and 65 days. For your Jackapoo, you should expect a gestation period lasting about 60 to 63 days. Once the female becomes pregnant, the pregnancy can be confirmed as early as 21 days after conception but it is usually best to wait for an exam until 28 days after.

2.) The Breeding Process

When your female Jackapoo goes into heat, she will display several of the following signs:

- A clear or pinkish discharge from the vulva – typically light in smaller dogs, heavier in full-size poodles.
- Swelling of the vulva
- Restlessness, may attempt to escape the house.
- Increase in urination

During her heat cycle, the female dog will also give off pheromones that will be highly attractive to male dogs. An intact male dog can smell a female dog in heat up to 3 miles (4.83 kg) away. For this reason, you need to be extremely careful when taking your dog outside – it is best to avoid taking her into public areas where other dogs may be present. During her heat cycle, the female may experience some pain or discomfort so she might need to retreat to a quiet, warm place – make sure to provide one for her.

It is generally recommended that you wait until the second week of a female's cycle to attempt breeding. The female will only be receptive to mating for a period of 5 to 8 days, so keep an eye on her behavior to determine when it is time for mating. Mating behavior varies from one breed to another, but for the most part the male mounts the female from behind and ejaculates his sperm into her. If the eggs become fertilized, conception will occur and the female will become pregnant. In pregnancy, the puppies will develop in the female's womb for a period of 59 to 63 days, in most cases (the length varies by breed).

It is important to keep track of when your female becomes pregnant so you can track the gestation period. By 21 days after conception the fetuses will attach to the uterine wall and, by 28 days, a qualified veterinarian will be able to feel the pups by palpating the female's abdomen. During the first few weeks of pregnancy you do not need to change how you care for your Jackapoo – normal feeding and exercise is recommended. As the female grows, however, you will need to cut back on exercise a bit.

By the fifth or sixth week of pregnancy, your Jackapoo female should start to look obviously pregnant. By the seventh week she may seem ready to explode but over the next two weeks her belly will grow tighter and harder. During the last week of pregnancy, the female's nipples will become larger and she may begin to lactate. You may need to feed her a bit more during the last few weeks of pregnancy, but be careful not to overfeed her. A diet consisting of high-quality protein, animal fat, and plenty of calcium is recommended.

3.) Raising the Puppies

By the eighth week of pregnancy, you need to start preparing for the puppies. Begin taking your Jackapoo's internal temperature on a regular basis – the normal temperature for a dog is between 100° and 102°F (37.7° to 38.8°C). About 24 hours before your Jackapoo starts to have contractions, her body temperature will drop by several degrees – sometimes as low as 98°F (36.6°C). At this time the female will also find a place to nest – somewhere quiet, dark, and warm – to deliver her puppies.

To make sure your female doesn't end up hiding somewhere you can't find her, it is a good idea to provide a nesting box during the last week of pregnancy. A nesting box can consist of a large box lined with newspaper or old rags – something you don't mind throwing away after the birth. During this last 24 hours you need to keep a close eye on the dog – do not let her go outside unattended and make sure she stays close to the nesting box.

As your female Jackapoo starts to go into labor, she may display signs of increasing discomfort. She may start moving restlessly and panting, frequently changing positions, even lying on her back. This stage of labor could last for several hours. In most cases, dogs prefer to give birth at night, so keep a close eye on her as night falls. Labor contractions occur in intervals of 10 minutes, usually in waves of three to five before a period of rest. If the female experiences two hours of contractions with no puppies being whelped, contact your veterinarian immediately.

For the most part, once the deliver begins the puppies will be delivered every half hour or so after between 10 and 30 minutes of forceful straining. After each puppy is born, the dam will lick it clean and bite off the umbilical cord. You must let the dam lick the puppies because it stimulates breathing and helps to get their blood circulating. After all of the puppies have been born, the dam will expel the remaining placenta and the puppies will begin to suckle – it is important that the pups suckled within 1 hour of being born to make sure they get some of the colostrum. The colostrum is the first milk produced by the dam and it contains vital nutrients and antibodies to protect the pups until their immune system develops. After giving birth, the dam will be very hungry so be prepared to give her as much food as she wants.

For the first few weeks after birth, it will seem like all the puppies do is sleep and nurse. The puppies are born with their eyes and ears closed, but both will open around 3 weeks of age. Between weeks 3 and 6 the puppies will start to play with each other and they will grow very quickly as long as the dam produces enough milk. Weaning should begin by week 6 and the mother will often do this automatically. During this time, provide the puppies with some solid puppy food that has been soaked in water to make it easier to digest.

By 8 weeks of age the puppies should be fully weaned and they will start to become more independent as well. This is the time when you can completely separate the puppies from their mother and you can begin to look for owners for the puppies. It is okay to bring in people to see the puppies before they reach 8 weeks of age but you should never separate a puppy from its mother before it is fully weaned. By week 10, your puppy's teeth will start to grow in so keep plenty of chew toys on hand.

Chapter Seven: Keeping Jackapoos Healthy

Providing your Jackapoo with a healthy diet and a clean environment are two of the most important factors in keeping him healthy. You should also cultivate a basic understanding of the various diseases to which your dog may be prone – in understanding these diseases you can quickly identify symptoms and get your dog the treatment he needs to recover quickly and fully.

1.) *Common Health Problems*

The fact that Jackapoos are a crossbreed may mean that they are less prone to certain congenital conditions that purebred dogs. It only makes sense because a shallow gene pool (the result of inbreeding) makes congenital conditions more likely – Jackapoos actually draw from two separate gene pools so they are less likely to inherit serious health problems. This does not make them immune to disease, however – there are still plenty of conditions which may affect your Jackapoo.

The following diseases and disorders are common in either the standard poodle or Jack Russell terrier and therefore may affect the Jackapoo as well:

- Addison's Disease (Poodle)
- Cataracts (Poodle)
- Cardiomyopathy (Jack Russell)
- Gastric Dilation Volvulus (Poodle)
- Glaucoma (Jack Russell & Poodle)
- Hip Dysplasia (Poodle)
- Legg-Calve-Perthes Syndrome (Jack Russell & Poodle)
- Lens Luxation (Jack Russell)

- Patellar Luxation (Jack Russell & Poodle)
- Von Willebrand's Disease (Jack Russell & Poodle)

In the following pages you will receive an overview of each of the ten diseases listed above. Included in this overview are the causes of the disease as well as symptoms and treatment options. The more you know about the diseases to which your Jackapoo may be prone, the better you will be able to diagnose them if they arise. Prompt diagnosis is the key to early treatment which gives your Jackapoo a greater chance of making a full recovery.

Addison's Disease

Breed Affected: Poodle

Also known as hypoadrenocorticism, Addison's Disease is caused by insufficient production of adrenal hormones by the adrenal gland. There are two different types of the disease – primary or secondary. Primary Addison's Disease affects the salt/potassium balance in your dog's body while secondary Addison's Disease only affects glucocorticoids. Some of the most common signs of this disease include vomiting, loss of appetite, and lethargy. Because these symptoms are fairly vague, Addison's Disease is very easy to miss until severe problems like shock, heart stoppage, or sudden death occur.

Treatments for Addison's Disease vary greatly depending on the type and the severity. If the dog suffers from fluid imbalance then IV fluids may be administered. In most cases, hormone replacement treatments are needed for the rest of the dog's life. This condition can be managed but the dog may forever be more sensitive to things like travel and hospitalization – more hormones may be needed in cases like these.

Cataracts

Breed Affected: Poodle

Cataracts are an eye problem that commonly affect the poodle breed, particularly toy poodles. This condition results from disease, old age, or trauma to the eye – it can also be an inherited condition. A cataract is actually an opacity in the lens of the eye which causes the dog to experience blurred vision. If the cataract is left untreated, it may slip out of plate and float around the eye, causing blockages that could lead to glaucoma and permanent blindness. In some cases, the cataracts dissolve slowly, causing painful inflammation.

Cataracts can be treated, though the treatment may vary from one case to another. If the dog has experienced vision loss, it may be repaired through surgery to remove and replace the lens with a plastic or acrylic substitute. There is generally a high success rate for cataract surgery, but dogs do require some extensive postoperative care and their rehabilitation may be slowed if they suffer from an underlying condition like diabetes.

Cardiomyopathy

Breed Affected: Jack Russell

Cardiomyopathy is a form of heart disease that may involve weakening of the heart muscle, thickening of the heart walls, or dilation of the chambers of the heart. Dilated cardiomyopathy (DCM) is one of the most common forms of cardiomyopathy and the risk for this disease increases with the dog's age. Common symptoms of this disease include anorexia, lethargy, rapid breathing, coughing, abdominal distention, and loss of consciousness. Unfortunately, the cause of this disease is unknown but it may result from nutritional deficiency or genetic inheritance.

Treatment options for dilated cardiomyopathy are aimed at improving the function of the heart and on treating symptoms of congestive heart failure. Medical treatments may help to slow rapid heartbeat and diuretics may help to control fluid buildup in the lungs. This disease is serious but entirely manageable, though regular check-ups are needed to monitor the dog's condition.

Gastric Dilation Volvulus

Breed Affected: Poodle

Also referred to as GDV, gastric dilation volvulus is a life-threatening condition that results from increased pressure and size of the stomach which causes torsion of the stomach. If your dog eats a mean too large or if he eats too quickly, it could result in gas that causes the stomach to expand – as pressure increases in the stomach, blood flow to the heart may be cut off and the stomach wall may even rupture. This is a very serious and life-threatening condition that requires immediate medical treatment.

Signs of GDV may include looking at the abdomen after a large meal, drooling, distended abdomen and non-productive retching. Your dog may also begin to pain and he may collapse. Emergency treatment is required to decompress the stomach by passing a tube down the esophagus to release air and flush food particles out of the stomach. In extreme cases, surgery may be required to de-rotate the stomach or to remove part of the stomach wall if it has become damaged.

Glaucoma

Breed Affected: Jack Russell and Poodle

Glaucoma is an eye condition in which too much pressure builds up in the eye, causes inadequate fluid drainage. If the pressure persists or becomes chronic, it may result in damage to the dog's optic nerve which typically causes total loss of vision. Approximately 40% of dogs affected by glaucoma lose vision in the affected eye within 1 year of developing the disease, regardless of treatment.

Symptoms of glaucoma include increased pressure in the eye, excessive blinking, redness of the vessels in the eye, cloudy appearance of the eye, dilated pupil, and vision loss. In advanced cases, you may also notice enlargement of the eye or degeneration within the eye itself. There are several medical treatments available for glaucoma to help lower pressure within the eye. If the condition has persisted for the long-term, damage to the optic nerve has likely already occurred and surgery may be required. If the condition results in loss of vision or loss of the eye, most dogs adjust well over time.

Hip Dysplasia

Breed Affected: Poodle

Hip dysplasia is a very common condition that primarily affects large-breed dogs, though it can affect other breeds as well. This disease is the result of the femoral head slipping out of the hip joint located on the pelvis. This is commonly connected to abnormal joint structure or laxity of the muscles responsible for keeping the femoral head in place. Though this disease most commonly affects adult dogs, it can be seen in puppies as young as 5 months.

Symptoms of hip dysplasia include pain and discomfort during and after exercise, difficulty walking, hopping or limping, stiffness in the leg, and eventual lameness. There are several surgical options available for the treatment of hip dysplasia depending on the progression of the disease as well as the age and size of the dog. In some cases a surgery is performed to fuse the pelvic bones together and in other cases a total hip replacement is necessary. Managing your dog's weight and encouraging regular exercise can help to prevent the disease.

Legg-Calve-Perthes Syndrome

<u>Breed Affected</u>: Jack Russell and Poodle

Sometimes referred to as LCPD, Legg-Calve-Perthes Syndrome occurs when the head of the femur bone degenerates, resulting in the degeneration of the hip joint as well – this is also accompanied by inflammation of the bone and joint. The cause for this disease is unknown, though it is likely related to blood supply problems to the femoral head. This disease is most common in miniature and small-breed dogs between 5 and 8 months of age.

Symptoms of Legg-Calve-Perthes Syndrome include gradual onset of lameness in the leg, carrying of the affected limb, pain in motion, and wasting of the thigh muscles. Diagnosis is typically made through examination of medical history and the dog's frequency of symptoms. In most cases, surgery is required to correct the problem and pain killers and cold packing may help to treat lameness prior to surgery. After surgery, physical therapy is needed to rehabilitate the limb.

Lens Luxation

<u>Breed Affected</u>: Jack Russell

Lens luxation is an inherited condition in which the lens of the eye moves out of its proper place. This condition is most commonly seen in adult dogs between 4 and 9 years of age, especially mixed-breed terriers. The symptoms of lens luxation may include reddening of the eye, swelling, pain, trembling of the lens, and trembling of the iris. Though this disease is primarily congenital, it may also result secondary to a tumor in the eye or trauma to the eye.

The treatment options for lens luxation vary from one case to another. If the affected dog still has partial vision, the lens may be removed surgically. In some cases, a special type of therapy may be used to keep the lens in place behind the pupil. If the dog has an irreversible loss of vision, the whole eye may be surgically removed and replaced with an artificial eye. This is the best option in cases where lens luxation is secondary to eye cancer.

Patellar Luxation

<u>Breed Affected</u>: Jack Russell and Poodle

Patellar luxation is a fairly common condition that involves the luxation, or slipping out of joint, of the patella (kneecap). The bones and joints of the leg are arranged so that the kneecap is held in place by ligaments over a groove in the femur – if the patella slips out of place, it may cause pain and eventual lameness. While patellar luxation may be inherited, it can also be caused by injury or deformity. This disease is most common in small and miniature breeds.

There are four different grades of patellar luxation. The first is intermittent – the patella slips out of place intermittently and returns easily to its proper place. The second is frequent patellar luxation in which the luxation is mostly permanent. Grade three is permanent patellar luxation in which the patella is luxated but the dog can still walk with the leg in a semi-flexed position. Grade four is permanent patellar luxation in which the dog walks in a crouched position with the limb partially flexed. Surgery is the most common and most effective method of treatment and, in 90% of cases, it prevents lameness and dysfunction.

Von Willebrand's Disease

Breed Affected: Jack Russell and Poodle

Sometimes simply referred to as vWD, von Willebrand's disease is an inherited bleeding disorder that results in abnormal platelet function and prolonged bleeding, even after minor injury. This disease is caused by dysfunction of or reduced amount of von Willebrand factor (vWF). There is a DNA test available for this disease so responsible breeders can remove affected dogs from the breeding stock to prevent the spread of vWD.

The most common symptoms of von Willebrand's disease is prolonged or profuse bleeding after minor injury, bleeding gums, nosebleeds, and blood in the urine. Unfortunately, there is no cure for von Willebrand's disease and affected dogs may require blood transfusions if a sufficient amount of blood is lost. In order for a dog to develop vWD, both parents must carry the gene. If your Jackapoo was bred from a poodle and a Jack Russell that are carriers for the disease, he has a good chance of developing it.

2.) Preventing Illness

Providing your Jackapoo with a healthy diet will go a long way toward preserving his health and well-being. There are a few other things you should do, however, to make sure that he stays healthy. You should plan to take your Jackapoo to the veterinarian twice per year (about every 6 months) for a general check-up and dental exam. During this check-up, your veterinarian will take your Jackapoo's weight, give him a physical exam, and check his teeth. Your vet may also take blood work or perform other tests to rule out certain conditions to which your dog may be prone.

Perhaps the most important thing you can do to preserve your Jackapoo's health is to have him vaccinated. There are a few vaccines that are recommended for all dogs while others are only recommended if you live in an area that is a high risk or if your dog has been exposed to the disease. Because requirements vary from one region to another, consult your veterinarian regarding the vaccines your Jackapoo really needs.

For the most part, however, the following vaccine schedule is recommended for dogs:

Recommended Vaccination Schedule			
Vaccine	**Doses**	**Age**	**Booster**
Rabies	1	12 weeks	annual
Distemper	3	6-16 weeks	3 years
Parvovirus	3	6-16 weeks	3 years
Adenovirus	3	6-16 weeks	3 years
Parainfluenza	3	6 weeks, 12-14 weeks	3 years

Bordatella	1	6 weeks	annual
Lyme Disease	2	9, 13-14 weeks	annual
Leptospirosis	2	12 and 16 weeks	annual
Canine Influenza	2	6-8, 8-12 weeks	annual

*Note: Remember, if you purchase a puppy from a breeder he may have already had some of his puppy shots. Make sure you get a health report and medical records from the breeder when you take your puppy home and bring them to your first vet appointment. Most breeders recommend taking your new puppy to the vet within 2 weeks of taking him home to make sure he stays on track with his vaccination schedule.

Chapter Eight: Showing Jackapoo Dogs

Because the Jackapoo is technically a hybrid breed, it is not recognized by the American Kennel Club (AKC), the UK Kennel Club or the Canadian Kennel Club. The Jackapoo is, however, recognized by several hybrid or crossbreed registries including the American Canine Hybrid Club, the Designer Dogs Kennel Club, the International Designer Canine Registry, and the Designer Breed Registry. In this chapter you will learn the basics about showing your Jackapoo in crossbreed dog shows.

1.) Showing Crossbreed Dogs

Because the Jackapoo is not recognized by the major kennel clubs, it cannot be shown in a traditional setting. There is, however, a large crossbreed show that occurs each year in the U.K. that you may be able to join. The world's largest dog show, Crufts, is held each year by the U.K. Kennel Club and they recently began holding a crossbreed competition called Scruffts in conjunction with the main show. This show is particularly designed for crossbreed dogs.

The Scruffts competition is not as formal or competitive as Crufts, but it is still a great opportunity for you to show your Jackapoo. In order to show your Jackapoo at Scruffts you must attend and pass through several heats that are held throughout the year in various locations around the U.K. The winners from each heat are invited to take part in the final round of competition in London. Then, the winners from each category are entered into the Scruffts competition which takes place at the same time as Crufts every year.

Because crossbreeds cannot be judged against each other in the same way that purebred dogs can, Scruffts utilizes a different form of judgment. <u>Dogs are invited to participate in one of six classes</u>:

- Child's Best Friend – puppies 6 to 12 months handled by a child 6 to 16 years old
- Most Handsome Dog – male dogs 6 months to 7 years old
- Prettiest Bitch – female dogs 6 months to 7 years old
- Golden Oldie – dogs 8 years and older
- Best Crossbreed Rescue
- Good Citizen Dog

While Scruffts may be the largest crossbreed dog show available, there may be other options open to you and your Jackapoo. Check the websites for the hybrid dog registries mentioned at the beginning of this chapter for upcoming show information.

2.) *What to Know Before Showing*

Before attending a dog show with your Jackapoo, there are a few things you need to know. Even though crossbreed shows may be more informal than a purebred competition, there is no reason that you can't take them seriously. <u>Below you will find tips for preparing your Jackapoo for show</u>:

- Make sure your Jackapoo is fully housetrained

- Your Jackapoo should be well socialized, able to get along with other dogs and humans in a competition setting

- Make sure your Jackapoo responds to basic commands and follows your lead

- Ensure that your Jackapoo is even-tempered and not hyperactive or unmanageable in public

- Make sure your Jackapoo meets the requirements for the show – each show has different requirements for age and other factors

- Take your Jackapoo to the vet before signing up for the show to make sure he is up to date on vaccinations

- Familiarize yourself with the rules of the competition to make sure you do not accidentally disqualify yourself or your Jackapoo

In addition to ensuring that your Jackapoo meets the requirements of the competition, you should also make some preparations for yourself. Below is a list of some of the items you may need to bring to the dog show. Consult the rules of the show to make sure there aren't any additional requirements or restrictions.

<u>Things to bring to a dog show</u>:

- Registration information
- Dog crate or exercise pen
- Grooming table and grooming supplies
- Food and treats
- Food and water bowls
- Trash bags
- Medication (if needed)
- Change of clothes
- Food/water for self
- Paper towels or rags
- Toys for the dog

Chapter Nine: Jackapoo Care Sheet

By the time you finish this book, you should have a firm understanding of the Jackapoo breed and you will be equipped with knowledge regarding Jackapoo care. In caring for your own Jackapoo, however, you may find that you need to reference key bits of information from time to time. Rather than flipping through the entire book, refer to this Jackapoo care sheet for the most relevant bits of information on your Jackapoo's diet, health, and breeding.

1.) Basic Information

Origins: unknown, likely developed in the United States

Pedigree: hybrid of the Standard Poodle and Jack Russell Terrier breeds

Weight: 12 to 25 lbs. (5.4 – 11.3 kg)

Height: average 10 to 15 inches (25.4 – 38 cm)

Lifespan: 12 to 15 years

Coat: may be smooth or rough in texture; either straight or curly; often medium-length

Colors: any color combination of white and tan is most commonly seen

Eyes: large and round; usually dark in color

Ears: medium-length, drop ears

Face: flat head, medium-length muzzle, un-tapered

Temperament: energetic, affectionate with family, alert and outgoing; generally good with kids; intelligent

Strangers: may be wary around strangers, make good watchdogs

Other Dogs: generally good with other dogs

Other Pets: strong hunting instincts, may not be good with small household pets

Training: very intelligent, responds well to firm and consistent training (best if started early)

Energy: fairly high exercise requirements; daily walk is required plus plenty of play time

2.) Cage Set-up Guide

Recommended Accessories: crate, dog bed, food/water dishes, toys, collar, leash, harness, grooming supplies

Collar and Harness: sized by weight

Grooming Supplies: slicker brush and wire pin brush

Grooming Frequency: brush several times a week; professional grooming 3 to 4 times a year

Energy Level: fairly high; bred from two hunting breeds

Exercise Requirements: at least 30 minutes per day plus playtime

Crate: highly recommended

Crate Size: just large enough for dog to lie down and turn around comfortably

Crate Extras: lined with blanket or plush pet bed

Food/Water: stainless steel bowls, clean daily

Toys: start with an assortment, see what the dog likes; include some mentally stimulating toys

Exercise Ideas: play games to give your dog extra exercise during the day; train your dog for various dog sports

3.) Nutritional Information

Nutritional Needs (Poodle): rich in animal protein, carbs/vitamins/minerals from plant sources, no processed grains

Nutritional Needs (Jack Russell): more protein and calories than other small breeds, protein from animal sources, carbs/vitamins/minerals from plants and grains

Nutritional Needs (Jackapoo): water; animal sources for protein and fats; plants for carbohydrate, vitamins, and minerals

Amount to Feed (puppy): feed freely but consult recommendations on the package

Amount to Feed (adult): consult recommendations on the package; calculated by weight

Important Ingredients: whole protein (chicken, beef, lamb, turkey, eggs), digestible carbohydrates (rice, oats, barley)

Important Minerals: calcium, phosphorus, potassium, magnesium, iron, copper and manganese

Important Vitamins: Vitamin A, Vitamin A, Vitamin B-12, Vitamin D, Vitamin C

Look For: AAFCO statement of nutritional adequacy

4.) Breeding Tips and Info

Sexual Maturity (male): as early as 5 months

Sexual Maturity (female): 6 to 12 months

Age of First Heat: around 6 months

Breeding Age (male): 9 to 12 months

Breeding Age (female): at least 12 months

Physical Maturity: about 12 months

Heat (Estrus) Cycle: 14 to 21 days

Frequency: twice a year, every 6 to 7 months

Greatest Fertility: 7 to 10 days into the cycle

Gestation Period (Poodle): 59 to 65 days

Gestation Period (Jack Russell): about 63 days

Gestation Period (Jackapoo): about 60 to 63 days (9 weeks)

Pregnancy Detection: possible after 21 days, best to wait 28 days

Signs of Labor: body temperature drops below normal 100° to 102°F (37.7° to 38.8°C), may be as low as 98°F (36.6°C); dog begins nesting in a dark, quiet place

Contractions: period of 10 minutes in waves of 3 to 5 followed by a period of rest

Whelping: puppies are born in 1/2 hour increments following 10 to 30 minutes of forceful straining

Litter Size: 4 to 8

Chapter Ten: Relevant Websites

This book is loaded with valuable information about the Jackapoo as well as the two parent breeds – the standard poodle and the Jack Russell Terrier. Even after reading this book, however, you may find that you still have questions or you need help finding the right food, toys, and accessories for your Jackapoo. In this chapter you will find a list of relevant websites for food and other accessories for your Jackapoo dog.

1.) Food for Jackapoo Dogs

United States Websites:

"Premium Nutrition Dog Food." Petco.
<http://www.petco.com/Shop/ShoppingGuides/petco_Choo
sePremiumDogFood_ShoppingGuideID_20_Nav_288.aspx>

"Dog Food Calculator." DogFoodAdvisor.
<http://www.dogfoodadvisor.com/dog-feeding-tips/dog-
food-calculator/>

"Natural Choice Dog Food for Medium-Sized Dogs."
Nutro. <http://www.nutro.com/natural-dog-food/natural-
choice-dog-food/medium-breed.aspx>

"Medium-Sized Dog Food." Royal Canin.
<http://www.royalcanin.us/products/products/dog-
products/size-health-nutrition/medium-dogs-from-23-55-
lb>

United Kingdom Websites:

"Dry Dog Food." Sainsbury's.
<http://www.sainsburys.co.uk/shop/gb/groceries/pet/dry-dog-food#langId=44&storeId=10151&catalogId=10122&categoryId=12309&parent_category_rn=12298&top_categor y=12298&pageSize=30&orderBy=FAVOURITES_FIRST&sea rchTerm=&beginIndex=0

"Blue Buffalo Natural Dog Food." BlueBuffalo.co.uk.
<http://bluebuffalo.com/?utm_referrer=bluebuff.co.uk>

"Breed and Size Specific Dog Nutrition." The Kennel Club.
< http://www.thekennelclub.org.uk/getting-a-dog-or-puppy/general-advice-about-caring-for-your-new-puppy-or-dog/feeding-your-puppy-or-dog/breed-and-size-specific-dog-nutrition/>

"Pet Nutrition Consultation." Pets at Home.
<http://www.petsathome.com/shop/en/pets/content/dog-nutrition-consultations?cm_re=Homepage-_-Service7-_-DOGNUTRITION-_ >

2.) *Toys and Accessories for Jackapoo Dogs*

United States Websites:

"Dog Grooming Supplies." PetsMart.
<http://www.petsmart.com/dog/grooming-supplies/cat-36-catid-100016>

"Dog Toys: Maximize Fun and Learning for Dogs." Drs.
Foster and Smith. < http://www.drsfostersmith.com/dog-supplies/dog-toys/ps/c/3307/3>

"Toys for Dogs." Entirely Pets.
<http://www.entirelypets.com/dogtoys.html >

"Dishes and Bowls." Drs. Foster and Smith.
<http://www.drsfostersmith.com/dog-supplies/feeders-waterers-and-bowls/dishes-and-bowls/ps/c/3307/15/90>

United Kingdom Websites:

"Dog Toys." PetPlanet.co.uk.
<http://www.petplanet.co.uk/dept.asp?dept_id=16>

"Stainless Steel Dog Bowls." ZooPlus.
<http://www.zooplus.co.uk/shop/dogs/dog_bowls_feeders/
stainless_steel_bowls>

"Dog Furniture." The Refined Canine.
<http://www.therefinedcanine.com/>

"Dog Bowls and Feeders." PetPlanet.co.uk.
<http://www.petplanet.co.uk/category.asp?dept_id=528>

"Wholesale Pet and Grooming Supplies." Ryan's Pet
Supplies. <http://www.ryanspet.com/ >

3.) General Info for Dog Care

United States Websites:

"Why You Should Never Buy a Puppy Online." ASPCA.org. < https://www.aspca.org/fight-cruelty/puppy-mills/why-you-should-never-buy-puppy-online>

"Pet Care Center: Dog." PetMD. <http://www.petmd.com/dog/petcare>

"Dog Care and Behavior." The Humane Society of the United States. <http://www.humanesociety.org/animals/dogs/tips/>

"Dog Training Tips." Nylabone. <http://www.nylabone.com/dog-101/training-behaviors/dog-training-tips/>

"Where to Get A Puppy." The Humane Society of the United States. <http://www.humanesociety.org/issues/puppy_mills/tips/buying_puppy.html >

United Kingdom Websites:

"Before You Look for a Puppy or Dog." The Kennel Club.
<http://www.thekennelclub.org.uk/getting-a-dog-or-
puppy/>

"Puppy and Dog Training Tips." A.P.D.T.
<http://www.apdt.co.uk/dog-owners/puppy-dog-training-
tips>

"Dog Welfare – Tips, Advice and Health." RSPCA.
<http://www.rspca.org.uk/adviceandwelfare/pets/dogs>

"General Advice About Caring for your New Puppy." The
Kennel Club. < http://www.thekennelclub.org.uk/getting-a-
dog-or-puppy/general-advice-about-caring-for-your-new-
puppy-or-dog/>

"Advice for Dog Owners." Merial.co.uk.
<http://www.merial.co.uk/Dog/Pages/advice_dogs.aspx>

Index

A

AAFCO · 55, 56, 99, 119

accessories · 24, 101

accidents · 27

activity · 44, 51, 52, 54, 57

Addison's Disease · 75, 77

Adenovirus · 88

age · 5, 21, 32, 43, 45, 57, 65, 66, 72, 78, 79, 82, 83, 84, 93

agility · 7, 10, 17, 32, 52

allergens · 57

American Canine Hybrid Club · 90

American Kennel Club · 3, 90, 122

apartment · 10

appearance · 9, 10, 18, 48, 81

B

Bordatella · 89

bowls · 27, 40, 42, 48, 94, 98, 104, 105

breed · 1, 2, 3, 5, 6, 7, 8, 13, 14, 15, 16, 18, 19, 25, 28, 32, 33, 35, 48, 51, 53, 54, 58, 64, 65, 66, 68, 78, 82, 83, 84, 90, 95, 102, 103, 122, 123

breeder · 13, 20, 24, 26, 34, 35, 36, 37, 38, 43, 45, 89, 121

breeding · 3, 4, 5, 8, 9, 36, 37, 64, 65, 66, 68, 86, 95

brush · 50, 97

C

cage · 47

calories · 54, 58, 98

cancer · 84

Canine Influenza · 89

carbohydrates · 54, 99

Cardiomyopathy · 79

care · 2, 6, 20, 24, 28, 29, 69, 78, 95, 120

care sheet · 95

Cataracts · 75, 78

characteristics · 1, 7

chewing · 27

children · 16, 18, 32, 33

cleaning products · 30, 40

coat · 3, 4, 10, 16, 18, 32

collar · 26, 49, 97

colors · 3, 10, 18

colostrum · 72

conception · 66, 68, 69

condition · 5, 37, 43, 77, 78, 79, 80, 81, 82, 84, 85

congenital · 9, 32, 36, 75, 84

contractions · 70, 71

cost · 24, 25, 26, 28, 29, 30, 65

crate · 24, 26, 27, 40, 42, 47, 50, 60, 61, 62, 63, 94, 97

Crufts · 91

cycle · 65, 66, 68, 99

D

dam · 3, 5, 71, 72

Designer Breed Registry · 90

Designer Dogs Kennel Club · 90

diagnosis · 76

diarrhea · 45

diet · 9, 53, 54, 59, 69, 74, 87, 95, 120, 123

discharge · 44, 67

diseases · 9, 25, 36, 74, 75, 76, 119

Distemper · 88

dog bed · 27, 47, 61, 97

dog food · 28, 55, 56

dog show · 7, 3, 91, 92, 93, 94

dog sports · 7, 9, 10, 15, 17, 32, 52, 58, 98

drooling · 80

E

ears · 4, 10, 11, 16, 18, 44, 72, 96

energy · 3, 9, 10, 15, 22, 33, 48, 50, 58, 59

exercise · 9, 10, 12, 15, 16, 18, 22, 33, 50, 52, 58, 69, 82, 94, 97, 98

F

family · 3, 4, 1, 2, 7, 11, 18, 32, 34, 63, 96

feeding · 53, 56, 58, 59, 69, 102, 103, 120

female · 3, 4, 65, 66, 67, 68, 69, 70, 71, 92, 99

flea and tick · 29

flyball · 7, 32, 52

food · 24, 27, 28, 40, 45, 46, 47, 48, 50, 53, 55, 56, 57, 58, 61, 72, 80, 97, 101, 102, 103

food label · 58

G

Gastric Dilation Volvulus · 75, 80

gestation period · 66, 68

Glaucoma · 75, 81

grooming · 28, 29, 32, 50, 94, 97, 104, 120

growth · 56, 57, 58

H

habitat · 46

harness · 47, 49, 97

healthy · 9, 32, 34, 35, 37, 43, 44, 45, 59, 74, 87, 120

heart · 77, 79, 80

heartworm · 29

heat · 50, 65, 66, 67, 68, 91

Hip Dysplasia · 75, 82

houseplants · 41

hunting · 7, 9, 12, 13, 14, 15, 17, 23, 32, 51, 97

hybrid · 7, 1, 7, 11, 25, 35, 53, 90, 92, 96

hypoallergenic · 18

I

identification · 21, 25

infection · 44

ingredients · 57

initial costs · 24

injury · 45, 85, 86

intelligence · 1, 9

International Designer Canine Registry · 90

J

Jack Russell terrier · 3, 1, 6, 7, 8, 16, 35, 51, 53, 75

L

labor · 71

lameness · 82, 83, 85

leash · 47, 49, 97

Legg-Calve-Perthes Syndrome · 75, 83

Lens Luxation · 75, 84

Leptospirosis · 89

lethargy · 77, 79

license · 20, 21, 28, 30

licensing · 19, 20

licensing requirements · 20

lifespan · 9

limping · 82

litter · 3, 7, 35, 37, 41, 65, 120

loss of vision · 81, 84

M

male · 4, 5, 65, 66, 68, 92, 99

mating · 4, 68

medications · 29, 40

mental stimulation · 16, 18, 22, 33, 48

microchipping · 24

minerals · 54, 55, 57, 98

miniature poodle · 17

monthly costs · 24, 28

mother · 3, 4, 21, 72, 73

N

nesting box · 71
nose · 10, 18, 44
nutritional needs · 46, 53, 55, 56

O

obedience · 17, 52
overfeeding · 58

P

pain · 68, 80, 82, 83, 84, 85
Parainfluenza · 88
parent · 1, 5, 6, 7, 8, 9, 13, 35, 36, 51, 53, 101, 103
Parvovirus · 88
Patellar Luxation · 76, 85
pheromones · 68
poodle · 3, 1, 6, 7, 8, 9, 10, 13, 17, 18, 29, 35, 49, 51, 53, 75, 78, 86,
    101, 115, 120, 121, 122
pregnant · 56, 64, 65, 66, 68, 69
problems · 43, 45, 75, 77, 83
pros and cons · 19, 32
protein · 53, 54, 55, 57, 58, 69, 98, 99
puppies · 3, 4, 21, 24, 35, 38, 39, 43, 44, 45, 48, 56, 58, 64, 65, 66, 68,
    70, 71, 72, 82, 92, 100
puppy · 2, 6, 25, 26, 27, 29, 34, 35, 37, 38, 39, 40, 41, 42, 43, 44, 45, 46,
    48, 49, 57, 62, 71, 72, 73, 89, 98, 103, 106, 107, 116, 119, 120, 121
purchase price · 24
purebred · 1, 3, 7, 9, 13, 25, 32, 75, 91, 93, 122

R

rabies · 21

recovery · 76

relevant websites · 101

rescue · 25, 38

S

Scruffts · 7, 91, 92

sexual maturity · 65, 66

sire · 3, 5

Small Dog Syndrome · 5, 10

socialization · 16, 43

spay/neuter surgery · 24, 25

stamina · 7, 9, 15, 51

surgery · 25, 78, 80, 81, 82, 83

swelling · 44, 84

symptoms · 44, 74, 76, 77, 79, 83, 84, 86

T

temperament · 2, 8, 16, 18, 44

temperature · 70, 100

toy poodle · 17

toys · 27, 30, 47, 48, 50, 73, 97, 98, 101, 104

train · 1, 9, 10, 15, 52, 61, 98

treatment · 74, 76, 78, 80, 81, 82, 84, 85

treats · 28, 56, 94

U

UK Kennel Club · 39, 90

V

vaccination · 21, 89
vaccine · 21, 88
veterinarian · 20, 25, 35, 38, 59, 69, 71, 87, 88
vitamins · 54, 55, 57, 98, 123
Von Willebrand's Disease · 76, 86

W

water · 13, 17, 27, 42, 47, 48, 50, 61, 72, 94, 97, 98
weaned · 43, 45, 72

Photo Credits

Cover Page Photo by Charlie and Tilly

Page 1 Photo By Genorama via Wikimedia Commons, <http://commons.wikimedia.org/wiki/File:Obi2920w.jpg>

Page 2 Photo By Charlie and Tilly

Page 15 Photo By Toupti1978 via Wikimedia Commons, <http://commons.wikimedia.org/wiki/File:Junior_jack_russe ll.jpg>

Page 17 Photo By HDP via Wikimedia Commons, <http://commons.wikimedia.org/wiki/File:Bo_the_poodle_r etrieving_a_duck.jpg>

Page 19 Photo By Karla Clippinger via Wikimedia Commons, <http://ja.wikipedia.org/wiki/%E3%83%97%E3%83%BC%E3 %83%89%E3%83%AB%E3%83%BB%E3%83%8F%E3%82% A4%E3%83%96%E3%83%AA%E3%83%83%E3%83%89#me

diaviewer/File:Second-
generation_cockapoo_puppy_(2006).jpg>

Page 34 Photo By Zuska via Wikimedia Commons,
<http://commons.wikimedia.org/wiki/Jack_Russell_Terrier#
mediaviewer/File:JRT_pixel_24-09-2010.jpg>

Page 46 Photo By Pleple2000 via Wikimedia Commons,
<http://commons.wikimedia.org/wiki/File:Pudel_miniatura
_342.jpg>

Page 55 Photo By Plank via Wikimedia Commons,
<http://commons.wikimedia.org/wiki/Jack_Russell_Terrier#
mediaviewer/File:Jack_Russell_Terrier_2.jpg>

Page 60 Photo By Jason Turse via Wikimedia Commons,
<http://commons.wikimedia.org/wiki/File:Apricot_Poodle,_
Roxy.jpg>

Page 64 Photo By Charlie and Tilly

Page 101 Photo By Golhen via Wikimedia Commons, <http://commons.wikimedia.org/wiki/File:Jack-Russell_Terrier.jpg>

References

"10 Ways to Puppy-Proof Your Home." PawNation
Animals. < http://www.pawnation.com/2013/09/09/puppy-
proof-your-home/1>

"13 Most Common Diseases Found in Jack Russell
Terriers." Dog Notebook. <http://www.dognotebook.com/
13-most-common-diseases-found-in-jack-russell-terriers/>

"AAFCO Dog Food Nutrient Profiles." DogFoodAdvisor.
<http://www.dogfoodadvisor.com/frequently-asked-
questions/aafco-nutrient-profiles/>

"Age of Sexual Maturity in Dogs." PetEducation.com.
<http://www.peteducation.com/article.cfm?c=2+2109&aid=1
027>

"An Owner's Guide to Poodles." Wmawhiney.
<http://wmawhiney.hubpages.com/hub/An-Owners-Guide-
to-Poodles>

"Breeding Your Bitch." FarmCliff Jack Russell Terriers.
<http://www.farmcliff.com/articles/Breeding%20Your%20Bi
tch.html>

"Choosing a Healthy Puppy." WebMD.
<http://pets.webmd.com/dogs/guide/choosing-healthy-puppy>

"Choosing a Puppy from a Litter." ASPCA.org.
<https://www.aspca.org/pet-care/virtual-pet-behaviorist/dog-behavior/choosing-puppy-litter>

"Dog Grooming Cost." Cost Helper.
<http://pets.costhelper.com/dog-grooming.html>

"How to Feed Your Jack Russell Terrier the Proper Diet and Nutrition." Petbrosia.com. <http://petbrosia.com/feeding-your-jack-russell-terrier-dog-diet-nutritional-needs/>

"Does a Poodle Have to be Groomed Like a Poodle?" Grooming Your Furry Friend.
<http://groomingyourfurryfriend.blogspot.com/2012/05/does-poodle-have-to-be-groomed-like.html>

"Health Issues in Poodles." The Poodle Club of America.
<http://www.poodleclubofamerica.org/all-about-poodles/health-concerns>

"How to Feed Your Poodle the Proper Diet and Nutrition." Petbrosia.com. <http://petbrosia.com/standard-poodle-diet-and-feeding/>

"How to Find a Responsible Dog Breeder." The Humane Society of the United States. <http://www.humanesociety.org/issues/puppy_mills/tips/finding_responsible_dog_breeder.html>

"Jack A Poo." Dog Breed Plus. <http://www.dogbreedplus.com/dog_breeds/jack_a_poo.php>

"Jack-A-Poo." Dog Breed Info Center. <http://www.dogbreedinfo.com/jackapoo.htm>

"Jack-a-Poo." DogsDiscovered.com. <http://dogsdiscovered.com/poodle-mixes-from-a-z/jack-a-pooalso-known-as-jackadoodle-jack-a-doodle-poo-jack-poojack>

"Jack-a-Poo Information." Great Dog Site. <http://www.greatdogsite.com/hybrids/details/Jack-A-Poo/>

"Jackapoo – Jack Russell Poodle Mix." Jack Russell Lover.com. <http://www.jack-russell-lover.com/jackapoo.html>

"Jack Russell Terrier." DogTime.com. <http://dogtime.com/dog-breeds/jack-russell-terrier>

"Medical: Caring for Your Jack Russell." Jack Russell Terrier Club of America. <http://www.therealjackrussell.com/breed/medical.php>

"Mixed Mutts and Designer Crosses: Healthier Than Purebred Pets?" VetStreet. <http://www.vetstreet.com/our-pet-experts/mixed-mutts-and-designer-crosses-healthier-than-purebred-pets>

"Poodle." American Kennel Club. <https://www.akc.org/breeds/poodle/index.cfm>

"Poodle." DogTime.com. <http://dogtime.com/dog-breeds/poodle>

"Poodle Breeding." The Poodle Information Center. <http://www.allpoodleinfo.com/Breeding_Poodles.html>

"Poodle Heat." The Poodle Information Center. <http://www.allpoodleinfo.com/Heat.html>

"Puppy Proofing Your Home." PetEducation.com. <http://www.peteducation.com/article.cfm?c=2+2106&aid=3283>

"Seasons/Heat Cycle." Love Jack Russells.
<http://lovejackrussells.com/forum/viewtopic.php?f=20&t
=8>

"The History of the Jack Russell Terrier." Jack Russell
Terrier Club of America.
<http://www.therealjackrussell.com/breed/history.php>

"Vitamins and Minerals Your Dog Needs." Kim Boatman.
The Dog Daily. <http://www.thedogdaily.com/dish/diet/
dogs_vitamins/index.html#.VHOtMPnF_IA>

"Whelping Puppies." FarmCliff Jack Russell Terriers.
<http://www.farmcliff.com/articles/Whelping-
Puppies.html>

Printed in Great Britain
by Amazon